The Last Street Before Cleveland

T0374683

CLASS IN AMERICA
Series Editor: *Jeffrey R. Di Leo*

The Last Street Before Cleveland

An Accidental Pilgrimage

Joe Mackall

University of Nebraska Press

Lincoln and London

Library of Congress Cataloging-in-Publication-Data
Mackall, Joe.
The last street before Cleveland : an accidental
pilgrimage / Joe Mackall   p. cm. – (Class in America)
ISBN-13: 978-0-8032-3255-6 (cloth : alkaline paper)
ISBN-10: 0-8032-3255-1 (cloth : alkaline paper)
ISBN-13: 978-0-8032-5474-9 (paper : alkaline paper)
1. Mackall, Joe. 2. Working class – Ohio – Cleveland –
Biography. 3. Catholics – Ohio – Cleveland – Biography.
4. Ex-church members – Catholic Church –
Biography. 5. Depression, Mental. 6. Cleveland
(Ohio) – Biography. I. Title. II. Series
CT275.M1365A3 2006 977.1'32043'092–dc22
2005022823

To my dad, Jim Mackall, and to the memory of
my mom, Chris (Gervasi) Mackall (1934–79)

It looked . . . like a place where people lived – a place where the difficult, intricate process of living could sometimes give rise to incredible harmonies of happiness and sometimes to near-tragic disorder . . . a place where it was possible for whole summers to be kind of crazy, where it was possible to feel lonely and confused in many ways and for things to look pretty bleak from time to time, but where everything, in the final analysis, was going to be all right. —Richard Yates, *Revolutionary Road*

I know nothing except what everyone knows – if there when Grace dances, I should dance. —W. H. Auden

1

We pull through the gates of Holy Cross Catholic Cemetery and park at the curb. Bobby – a complete stranger to me until fifteen minutes ago – knows the location of Tom's grave because of a water pipe sticking up among the gravestones. It's nice to know my old friend had somebody in his final days.

His final days.

Makes it sound as if Tom died in bed, covered by crisp and clean home-worn sheets in the last days of his eightieth year after a good long life full of love and success, modest failures and seasoned pain, where grandchildren filled long Sunday afternoons crawling up on his aching knees as he dreamed of the long-ago kiss under a black umbrella in a light rain from a girl whose name still brings a small, sweet smile to his lips.

But no.

Tom (aka the Ragman) was thirty-seven years old when he died. On a hot August afternoon in 1997 Bobby found him furled up cold, alone, and dead in the front seat of a used Buick in a run-down neighborhood.

"It's right here," Bobby says, using his boot to brush snow off the Ragman's stone, which is between the paid-in-full but still empty grave sites of his parents. Bobby crosses himself and says a quick prayer over the Ragman.

Suddenly I have the feeling that I'm trespassing, that I have no right to be here. Surely some of these stones read Rest in Peace.

I too make the sign of the cross and bow my head as if in prayer, something I gave up forever on Valentine's Day 1979. Instead I look up at Bobby and observe a moment of real prayer, when a person full of faith prays for the lost soul of a close friend.

Bobby's eyes look sealed, shut tight against the cold. A jovial burly and bearded man in his early sixties, Bobby is bundled up in layers, and his clothes and the eyes closed in prayer combine to somehow diminish him or make him appear to be elsewhere, as if he has just left a room with the promise of coming right back.

We're close to my mother's grave, and suddenly I have the irrational thought that this is all some kind of ruse and Tom and this stranger have tricked me into praying over her.

My mom died at forty-four. My age as I stand in this cemetery.

"I'm going over here for a minute. I'll leave you alone," Bobby tells me as he heads to his own mother's grave site not fifty feet from Tom's. I watch him walk away. He slips on a headstone. The snow slickens the stones of the dead. Bobby looks down at the name carved into the gravestone he's slipped on, the way you might glance at the face of a person you accidentally bumped in a crowded department store at Christmastime.

When he reaches his mother's stone, Bobby crosses himself for the third time in five minutes and bows his head. I feel a sting of envy for his faith. I cross myself again, meaninglessly, and stare down at Tom's stone, which is decorated with stickers, colorful caricatures of buzzards. In the seventies and early eighties the buzzard was the symbol and the moniker of Cleveland's famous rock-and-roll station, WMMS. "In God's Loving Care" adorns the space not covered with the vultures of rock.

THOMAS MCGINTY, 1959–1997.

I lean down and push the snow out of Tom's life line, that tiny groove separating the date of his birth from that of his death. A train whistle splits the winter night. I want to feel more than I do. Granted, Tom and I were never very good friends, but because he lived on our street, he was one of us. And being one of us meant something. I want to pray and cry and pray and pound the earth

2

over these acres of stones, but I just focus on the grooves spelling out a life spent.

"Do you want to stop and see your mom?" Bobby asks. It's a nice thing to ask a relative stranger. I wish I could deliver on the other side of this niceness and take him up on it.

"No thanks. I stop around a lot," I lie.

The fact is I haven't been back much over the years, but as of late I've started dropping by. I'm coming back to the last street before Cleveland because I feel pulled back. For all practical purposes I left Cleveland – the place of my birth – in 1980. Since then I've lived in Washington DC, Georgia, Kentucky, Maryland, Oklahoma, and Virginia. I've been back in Ohio since 1990. Although for more than a decade I've lived happily sixty miles from this graveyard I once called a neighborhood, in the past couple of months I find myself here more and more.

I'll tell my wife I have errands to run and end up where I began, Fairlawn Drive. Or I'll get off the highway and deliberately wander into the square mile that was once my universe, driving up and down streets, through parking lots, looking, longing. And then I'll find myself parked on my childhood street, the last street before Cleveland, searching for tidbits of truth in the factory smoke and the sidewalks, in the brittle gait of retired auto workers or the wary eyes of cautious Catholics.

The last street before Cleveland is where I swore I'd never return. For it's there I spurned and abandoned my Catholic faith. There I rejected my blue-collar, working-class roots. There I jettisoned friends and distanced myself from family.

There is the last place I was truly whole.

The cold on this February night is bitter. It gets under your gloves and down in your boots, turns your nose red, your eyes teary.

I step toward the car, and I'm dizzy. I grab the hood, waiting for the vertigo to pass and trying not to slip and fall. Resident geese honk their antidirge. I pick a piece of hood ice free with my fingers.

And then suddenly they're all here. In this cemetery rest my mother, two sets of grandparents – an aunt here, an uncle there, a cousin totaled at twenty-one, an uncle murdered at forty-one. And somewhere, under the honks of graveyard geese, lies little Thomas John, a cousin whose entire life stretched all of an hour, all here now as branches weave in the winter wind and the snow falls. A stranger asks if I'm okay and I say yes, as the living visit the dead and the dead the living.

Tom shouldn't be one of the dead. Not this soon. If not foul play, the Ragman's death was most certainly foul. And there are others. Boys, now men – me included, maybe especially me – with "hearts as big as car engines," whose adult lives have been trouble: a series of marriages and divorces, one nowhere job after another, unemployment, trouble with alcohol and drugs, failed attempts at faith and love, parents who died too young, and parents who should have.

One was my mother, dead at forty-four, who took my faith with her to the grave.

Maybe I'm going back to Fairlawn Drive to find out what and who we were and what happened. What kind of men emerge from boys with hearts the size of internal combustion engines? How does a boy combust internally into a man? What explosions fire the cylinders of the human heart? What fuel does it burn? Surely a man's power derives from something more than gasoline vapor and air.

What happened to the person I thought I'd be?

Sure, that's it, I tell myself. That's it.

I couldn't be here because lately I've been haunted by my mother and Tom. Haunted by my mother's early death and Tom's drug-driven end. I know it's no coincidence that I've been pulled back

4

now of all times, now when I feel myself standing at the edge of sobriety and sanity, wondering whether I'll outlive my mother, fearing I'm destined to meet the same fate as Tom, wanting a drink or a drug more than at any time in the sixteen years I've been sober.

"Are you ready to get going?" Bobby asks, as he knocks the snow off his boots. "No hurry if you want to hang around."

No, you go on ahead. I'll stay here. In the snow. With my family. Thoughts like these tell me I need to understand the hold my past has on me.

So I tell Bobby I'm ready, and I too knock the snow off my boots, a salute to this stranger whom I have watched pray twice in fifteen minutes.

I take one last look at the Ragman's slick stone. I gaze in the direction of my mother's grave. It's out there too, somewhere in the snow and cold. I know the family and friends lying dead in this cemetery have all taken something of me with them.

I wonder how much more of me can be lost before I am substantially less.

On this, one of my first nights back in the old neighborhood, I'm still two years away from understanding that this was the moment from which all else would follow. I did not know then that I would leave the stones and cold of this night and begin the process of losing the life I'd been living.

2

Just short of the gleaming fifteen-foot-tall marble cross that blesses the entrance and exit of this cemetery cluttered with Catholic dead, Bobby stops the car as if he's forgotten something. "I've got a lot of my family back in there," he says.

I know I should encourage him to say what he has inside him. Maybe I should inquire about his family, let him talk, be a good listener, learn something about this stranger who has been my docent to the dead. I should help him mourn, provide the shoulder, but I just don't have it in me right now. "Yeah," I say. "Me too."

We sit silently for a moment, this stranger and I, stalled at the exit of this boneyard, looking out over the landscape surrounding us. Diagonally across from the cemetery is a strip joint, and past that is an establishment with adult "viewing" rooms and bookstores. Even on a Sunday evening, the porn parking lot is packed. The cold, the snow, and the neon lights break the graveyard night with promises of secret sex, creating the illusion that we've fallen into some kind of apocryphal hell where snakes bathe with kittens, pedophiles dance with Jerry's kids, and terrorists skip rope with soccer moms in obsidian school yards.

I'm pulled out of my dark reverie by Bobby's jerking the car out into the traffic of Brookpark Road. The rear end swerves into the next lane, and at that moment I don't give a damn if we bang steel and bone with other drivers. Let it happen.

Bobby masterfully maneuvers us back into our lane. I glance at the side-view mirror and catch sight of a shrinking cross standing sentry over the dead of my family, growing smaller with each piston pump of the engine.

As if my thoughts leaped out when the car slowed and sprinted back to the dead gates holding my blood, I think of my maternal grandfather, Cosimo Leo Gervasi, an immigrant alone in New York City at age twelve, never seeing his family again, hooking up with the wrong Italians, ones with nicknames like "the Executioner." My grandmother Anna (Donahue) Gervasi married at seventeen, eager to leave an abusive home and wed the fiery young man with the olive skin from a faraway place. On my father's side my grandpa Russell Mackall, once a coal miner in western Pennsylvania, for a stretch of his life saw the sun only on the Sabbath. He and my paternal grandmother, Marie (Casey) Mackall, waited ten years to marry because Russell wasn't Catholic. When they did marry, my great-grandmother refused to attend the wedding.

There's Uncle Joe, who fought in World War II and mailed a letter written by a dead German soldier to the fallen man's home. There's my cousin Jimmy, who loved cars more than anything on earth other than girls who loved boys who loved cars more than anything on earth. As a teenager wanting to hear music constantly, I once turned on the radio as I rode shotgun in his souped-up Dodge. He quickly shut it off. "I like to listen to the engine," he said. The engine's music carried him out of this world during a drag race one winter night. He was twenty-one. When I had to tell my dying mother of her nephew's violent death as she lay in her hospital bed in our home, she pulled the covers over her face and sobbed. There's my uncle Don, murdered one Friday the thirteenth. And there are others who own a piece of me as I do of them, all hanging out in a cemetery that extends for acres on the edge of the strip joints and porn shops that taper themselves blade sharp on the edge of Cleveland.

Bobby takes me back to my car. We have a quick cup of coffee at a Big Boy restaurant where it's obvious he's a regular. Customers wave. He nods. Some call out greetings. Words are exchanged. He knows everybody. When his girlfriend joins us, an attractive brunette who looks to be in her late fifties, I stay a polite length of time and then make my excuses.

The truth is that I want to drive the few miles back to the old neighborhood.

I'd be lying if I didn't admit to a little lightheadedness at this moment. Perhaps this touch of vertigo developed because my visit to the cemetery came after such a long absence – years in fact. Maybe it's because I can't shake thoughts of Tom, cold, dead, failed, and alone at thirty-seven, seven years younger than I am now.

When I truly focus again, my car has delivered me back on Fairlawn Drive, to the home of the Ragman, Tom McGinty, like a horse who takes its drunken, wounded, or unconscious rider home.

Tom lived at the dead end of our street, two houses up from the General Motors Chevy plant, where a good many of my friends' fathers worked – at least those who lived on the dead-end end. If they didn't work there, they worked at the Ford factory. Or at least that's how it seemed to me then.

What I remember most about these men is the way they moved – that and the topography of their hands. The blue-collar men of my youth lumbered; they walked always as if burdened. Burdened by tough physical labor, thirty-year mortgages, too many kids, bowing to the pope, living by the rules, wondering why it wasn't all working the way the big American promise said it would. It was as if they led with their backs. They led with their backs and fed their families with hands gray with embedded grease and dirt. Never since have I seen such muscular hands. One wouldn't have to be a seer or a charlatan to divine the past, present, and future in the palms of these men. It was all there, spelled out in dirt-filled seams and creases, permanent calluses, grit impossible to wash away, as much a part of them as the tolling of the factory's time clocks, their noise the sinews holding together muscle and bone, work and home.

The Chevy plant, with its smoke and noise and promises of good pensions, latent poisons, and two-week vacations, supplied one of the four borders – symbolic and actual – that enclosed our street, defined its possibilities. And, so it seemed then, that also enclosed and defined our lives.

The power of the plant was obvious. Its smoky productivity colored the dusk as the sun dropped behind its smokestacks. At times the sunsets were even more mysterious and beautiful because of the brilliant orange, dust-fuzzy pollution glow. Perhaps this is a kind of beauty only a blue-collar kid can perceive, just like the beauty inherent in exhaust fumes emitted from the tailpipe of a rusty beater on a frost-laden winter morning, the way the gas mutates into a smoky presence that rises and then disappears like incense offered at the Stations of the Cross on Good Friday afternoons.

Somewhere in the synapses of my brain or the tissues of my heart there somehow exists the notion (belief? desire?) that there is a spot reserved for me on the assembly line at Chevy, just waiting for me to take my rightful place, punch my time card, collect my pay. I'm bound to be found out. One day I expect the university provost and the factory foreman to walk into one of my writing classes, pull me out into the hall, and inform me that they're on to my ruse and that I'm expected to clock in for the graveyard shift.

I'm also missed at the bar at three o'clock every afternoon after the day shift, where a factory friend slaps the empty stool next to him so I'll sit down and have that beer. And at this bar these men – mostly white – will be joined by a black guy they work with on the line. They all laugh together and switch off buying rounds. And the men do not have to feel like racists, not here, not now. "Hell, if all blacks were like this guy, there'd be no race trouble in this country. I've got nothing against the blacks, I work with black guys. Hell, this one black guy even knocks back beers with us after our shift. I don't care if a guy's black or white or green or purple, if he does his job, he's okay with me." After drinks these men get in their bank-owned cars and drive the few minutes home, while the black guy drives to his home, not in this neat blue-collar suburb called Parma, but back to Cleveland. If a black family moved into the neighborhood, these same men would put their houses up for sale and flee. They've all been breast-fed on their parents' horror stories of bottom-dwelling real estate values after the epic era of white flight. All of our white parents and grandparents, aunts and uncles, fled Cleveland en masse. They fled to Parma, now recognized nationally as one of the most racist cities in the country, where the number of cross burnings in the past few years still exceeds the number of black police officers or firefighters. I have to wonder how much this setting contributed to the casual racism among us blue-collar babes, a racism as mindless and ignorant as our spitting contests and rock fights.

The temperature has dropped below twenty, and it's dark now in front of Tom's old house. Tom has somehow been reduced to a gravestone, a house he no longer lives in, and the official language of an autopsy report that spells out a life and a death.

A week earlier I had sat dazed, reading the report: Tom was born on August 29, 1959. He died at 4:39 p.m. on August 12, 1997. He was still thirty-seven, just fifteen days short of his thirty-eighth birthday. His death certificate lists his occupation as mechanic.

There is history that on August 12th, 1997 at about 2 p.m., the Cleveland Police and Emergency Medical Service responded to a call of a male down in an auto. On arrival, the said Thomas P. McGinty was found expired, seated in the front seat of a parked vehicle. The County Coroner's Office was notified and the Cuya-hoga Ambulance Company was dispatched. This man was then transported to aforementioned Coroner's office where he was pronounced dead at the aforementioned time and date and an autopsy was performed which revealed: acute intoxication by ethanol and drugs, and the Cleveland Police were notified. It was determined that on or about August 11, 1997 the said Thomas P. McGinty sustained self-administered overdose of ethanol and drugs, in an accidental fashion, in an unknown location in Cleve-land, Ohio, and subsequently expired in the aforementioned cir-cumstance. That death in this case was the end result of acute in-toxication by combined effects of amitriptyline and ethanol, and recent use of marijuana and cocaine, sustained in the aforemen-tioned circumstance, and was accidental in nature.

Blue eyes, brown hair, fair teeth, unshaven beard, brown mus-tache, medium complexion, 72 inches in height, weighed 180 pounds and was a mechanic. Marital status: Divorced.

Case number 228528 and autopsy number m-70144.

Anatomic Diagnoses:

Mild arteriosclerosis heart disease with: mild intramyocardial vascular sclerosis; mild perivascular myocardial fibrosis; mild periadrenal vascular sclerosis.

Early postmortem decomposition.

External Examination: The body is that of a well developed, well nourished white male of 37 years. . . . Rigor mortis is partial, remaining in the fingers and jaw and lividity of the trunk and face, and purple-pink fixed lividity posteriorly. The body temperature is cold. Early rigor mortis, cloudy cornea, slight green discolora-tion of the abdomen, and scattered areas of skin blistering and slippage.

The hair is brown, normal in amount, texture and distribu-tion. A brown mustache is present and the remainder of the face is clean shaven. Acne scars are noted in the face. The irises are blue, the sclerae are white, the corneae are cloudy, and the conjunctivae are congested without petechial hemorrhages. The ears, nose, and mouth show no injuries or abnormalities. The teeth are natural and in good condition. The neck is of normal configuration, and free of palpable masses. The chest, back and abdomen reveal no injuries or abnormalities. The external genitalia are those of a normal adult circumcised male. Both testicles are descended. The extremities show no joint deformities and all digits are present. Calluses are present on the plantar surface of both feet. The palmar surface of the hands shows gray-black staining. The skin shows acne lesions in the neck and gluteal region. Otherwise, the skin is of normal texture and pliability.

The exposed musculature is unremarkable . . . the heart is of normal configuration . . . heart valves are thin, pliable, delicate.

Tom's life has come down to a discussion of plantar and palmar surfaces.

For weeks after this, various phrases invade my head in the middle of the night or at the beginning of a class or when I'm saying good night to my kids: "self-administered overdose," "unknown location," "unremarkable musculature," "heart valves are thin, pliable, delicate."

It's almost as if Tom chose to die on a drug corner in Cleveland, a place rife with gaping holes that guys like him could easily fall into and disappear. He must have known he was falling; part of him must have chosen to fall. Perhaps it was easier for him to grab hold of booze, marijuana, cocaine, a failed antidepressant, then raise his arms high above his head, hold his breath, and rush down into the promise of sweet oblivion. In a world where the faint flapping of a butterfly's wings is said to stir hurricanes thousands of miles away, Tom's death disturbed not a wave or a particle. This is no sea change. This is no continental drift. Listless death. Unnoticed death. The death of a guy who was as easy to like as he was to pity.

I cup my fingers around my nose and blow out hot air to warm my frigid snout, which is always the first thing to go cold. I know I should drive by my childhood home, but I resist the impulse. No point in that, I tell myself. Nothing here has changed much. I need to return to my real home, where my wife waits and my children sleep.

I decide instead to at least peruse the outside of the Chevy plant before I leave. Under the night lights, the lawn in front of the plant offices looks a fresh chemical green, fostering the illusion that this is nothing more than a worker's home away from home. The light-brown brick facade is unchanged, as if a quarter of a century were a nanosecond. Soon I'm feeling depressed by bland brick and metal fences, the cheery signs of work and of my own tired and tiresome observations.

Once the plant becomes an image in my rearview mirror, I decide to visit St. Bridget's Church and School, where I spent kindergarten through eighth grade. St. Bees, as parishioners lovingly called it, was more than a church and a school. It was a religious city hall. It was the place we received the host on Sundays, ate our fried fish on Fridays, and confessed our sins through lies on late Saturday afternoons.

At ten o'clock on this Sunday night, the place is deserted. Nobody's guarding a runner at first or watching the left field line on Father Blair's ballpark. Nobody sprints along the sideline of the football field; no seventh-grade couple sits holding hands on a picnic table in the grove of trees across from the convent. No math gets scratched out on green blackboards, no phonics is practiced in classrooms. No unruly boy stands in the corner for hours beneath the statue of the Virgin Mary, the nuns hoping grace will descend on him like spiritual excrement, curing his stutter, curbing his poor behavior. The church sits empty. Nobody lights votive candles for a sick loved one. Not a soul kneels, then stands, then sits. No kid stares at the priest and imagines him vulnerable to a sniper's bullet. I am alone with my anger and doubt, my longing and nostalgia.

I want to know where my faith has gone and why I hopelessly ache for its return.

I roll down my window and breathe in the night. I catch my breath and inhale as deeply as I can, until my lungs start to burn the way they once burned with pesticide-laced pot. I inhale and exhale, inhale and exhale, until I fear I'll hyperventilate and pass out, as we used to coach a drunken friend into doing on Friday nights at the drive-in theater behind our street.

I stop the respiratory torture to collect my thoughts and find that what I suspect is true: the biting night air is not all I'm trying to breathe in. I'm aching to drag the past into my lungs. By some kind of dimension-defying desperation, I want to inhale the living knowledge of the long ago. Then I'll understand, I tell myself. Then it will all make sense.

Cold again from an open window and a dormant heater, I give up my quest to suck in a long-gone time. I close my window and start the engine, blasting the heat. Shaking my head at my capacity for idiotic wonder and childhood magic, I pull out of the parking lot of St. Bridget's Church and School, stopping only briefly to let my window down a couple of inches near the statue of the Virgin Mother, her open arms stretching down, welcoming all who enter.

And, I wonder, all who leave?

No doubt there's an empty space for me on one of the wooden pews of the church. The space is mine. I can almost feel the pain in my knees from the threadbare kneelers. Perhaps if I venture back to the room behind the altar I'll find my altar boy's white surplice and black cassock still hanging in the closet; I'll shed my lapsarian garb and slip into my costume and back into the faith. Just like that. As if Mass were just yesterday.

But I know these feelings must be nothing more than awareness that this square mile where the church is central owns me in a way no other place can or ever will. As Eudora Welty wrote, "The home tie is the blood tie. And had it meant nothing to us, any other place thereafter would have meant less, and we would carry no compass inside ourselves to find home ever, anywhere at all. We would not even guess what we had missed."

For twenty-five years I've resisted the magnetic north of home. I no longer can. I need to discover the ways my past is holding me back. Or perhaps the ways I'm still clinging to it. Growing up, it seemed that people were dropping dead all around me. Each death tugged me down deeper. I need to shake myself free of the dead hanging low from the family tree. Things I thought I'd shed forever – Catholicism, my working-class beginnings, dead friends and family – have begun a long, slow pull. And the person leading the tug-of-war is Tom.

I drive along the Metroparks system, which sits parallel to the Chevy plant. The park is a decently wooded area with bike trails and owl hoots, where we lost baseball after baseball, banged into the woods off aluminum bats by boys who still had only marginal control over their bodies' abilities or desires. We knew to avoid the restroom in the park that acted as a kind of lunch-box confessional for pasty and skin-heavy middle-aged men from somewhere else who huddled for anonymous gay sex. We spent hours at the creek bed, skipping stones, swinging out on vines, exploring our environment as if we were the first people here, talking about everything we didn't comprehend. It was also the place pubescent boys hid skin magazines in the trunks of dead trees. Later it was a nice place to walk a girl along a worn path and dream that we would all live a different and better life than our parents lived.

We were bred and conditioned to see the blue-collar lives of our parents and neighbors as something to leave behind, even to look down on, as we climbed to white-collar wealth and ease. But what did we lose? Whenever I see a group of men standing around a car with its hood up or by the open tailgate of a pickup on a weekday afternoon, I ache for a life no longer lived. I know the communion being offered and received beneath that hood as the men grind grease and shared experience into their skinned and bruised hands. These men made my youth go round. They could fix anything. They solved every mechanical mystery or malfunction. They prized their tools the way I imagine fourteenth-century knights prized their swords, maces, and halberds. It must have stunned them as it stunned me that by following all the rules and taking care with and of their tools, their cars, their lawns, their faith, their families, and by being able to restore any broken thing, they were teaching us to desire nothing more than to leave their world behind, to use their bent and beaten backs to climb higher, to use their brick-hard hands to get a boost, to use their lives as an impetus to seek a better one. This is their legacy.

My father, who worked as a bricklayer before and after his ten years as a Cleveland cop and later a homicide detective, has for nearly half a century now carried shards of brick in his fingers, tiny chips of progress buried under layers of skin.

For over twenty years I've been ashamed of my own scarred blue-collar skin. Working on a brick job with my father, I once walked through a footer that was filling with slow-moving cement to help push it along, because I was in a hurry to leave work and register for college classes. The blue-collar move in microcosm. Later that day, chemicals from the cement began eating away at my skin, causing second-degree burns. Scars still cover my calves. I hated these scars for years, physical evidence of a life I tried to forget. Lately I've been seeing them again, fingering the tiny arroyos in my skin as if they have a lesson to teach, a message to send.

Although my dad always wanted me to learn a trade to "fall back on," he insisted on my being the first of his line to attend college. Even before I knew I wanted college, he made it clear I had no choice in the matter. Too many Mackall men had given too much to body-hungry physical labor. I was taught to move on from it, to leave it behind, to reject the working-class life of our ancestors. But what is the cost of this wholesale rejection of a way of life?

Driving by my street, refusing to even glance at the rows of identical ranches I called home for eighteen years, I cross over Brookpark Road, which looms parallel to St. Bridget's. Brookpark is a busy four-lane packed with semis and with station wagons, pickup trucks, and cars made by the same men and women who drive them. Along both sides of Brookpark – the official start of Cleveland – are crammed gas stations, discount department stores, small businesses posting rare job openings, bar after bar with names like Anchor Inn and Third Shift Tavern, motel after gas station, strip joint after adult bookstore, all leading to the airport. The planes that incessantly flew over our heads to destinations we could only dream of took off and landed regardless of what we did or of any knowledge that we'd be dead at thirty-seven and our death would surprise nobody.

Perhaps Tom felt the same sense of something lost that I did, and living in the shadow of Cleveland fed this feeling. Being the civic manifestation of the nation's punch line did not sit well with Clevelanders' ethnic pride. Ironically, when pollution of air and water was the worst, there were also the most jobs. Cleveland's rust belt economy and mentality buoyed its people and encouraged their dreams.

Although Cleveland was founded by and named for soldier, lawyer, and frontiersman Moses Cleaveland, at least a vowel of his legacy was lost. According to local lore, an early Cleveland newspaper editor couldn't fit the original spelling of the city into a headline, so he took it upon himself to drop the first *a*. It always seemed to me that the missing *a* contained all that could have been good about the city of my birth. Maybe comedians wouldn't have been telling Cleveland jokes if the *a* and all the mystery it held had survived. Maybe the city wouldn't have defied the elements and the Cuyahoga River wouldn't have burned when I was eleven years old.

When water catches fire, loss is sure to follow.

We lived bordered by our possibilities. Would it be a working-class, blue-collar, overtime, debt-heavy, layoff-fearing life in the factory? The straight and narrow march of a good Catholic? Could the natural world of the Metroparks offer us refuge with its promises of epic overstories and understories? Or would it be a wild ride through the blue-collar commerce and flesh that society served and the church feared? Or perhaps we'd all be lifted away on the wings of education, or good luck or pluck, or stubbornness or ambition or want, which would take us up and away from Fairlawn Drive, the final northern street in the parish, the drive that bumped up against Cleveland, the last street off Queens Highway, home to the Ragman, Tom McGinty.

Home to me.

As I drive away from this square mile that owns me in ways I won't understand until over a year later, I am still utterly oblivious to what I'm about to go through and what this homecoming will end up costing me.

3

After my visit to the cemetery, my life basically returns to normal. My oldest daughter enters graduate school; my son settles into college; and my youngest daughter, in all her specialness, continues her vocational program. My wife, Dandi, writes her children's books, and I teach my writing classes at the university, knowing how good my life is as a tenured English professor, and a working writer and editor and wondering why I'm becoming disturbingly more miserable with each passing day.

Although the black dog of depression has been my loyal companion for years, this new darkness is different. I've been on antidepressant medication for nearly a decade, and it has worked. But it seems impotent against this fresh misery. For much of my twenties I worked and played at drowning the dog with alcohol, which worked until it didn't. I quit drinking and using drugs three weeks before my thirtieth birthday, determined not to enter another decade of working to put down the ebony canine.

So by two weeks after the cemetery visit, I've been sober for over fifteen years, medicated for nine. I love my wife, my marriage, my children, and my work, but daily I feel the hammering of an emptiness whose unrelenting pounding increases steadily with each new day.

And the worse I feel, the more I want to go back to the place I swore I'd never return to.

On my first daytime visit to the old neighborhood, my mood is as dark and gray, as listless – yet as volatile – as the sky. The first thing I look for is the detached and unnervingly pale mannequin's hand that seems to wave at me – or reach out for me – from the street's corner house. My friends and I believed the hand belonged to someone buried inside the rafters above the garage, sticking through the confines of her coffin, forever trapped behind (and beyond?) an octagon of glass.

Looked at another way, the hand, palm outward, is signaling me to stop. Maybe it's saying that there comes a time in life when a person stands still for the first time in twenty-odd years and asks, How did I get here?

Though I want to be hard on the boy who believed the world worked in such a literary way, I try to remember that he lived within several grand narratives. The Christian narrative had the poor and downtrodden saved and the rich having a difficult time finding their way to the ultimate reward. Nearly every book I read, and as a kid I read hundreds, seemed to echo this idea that the low will be on top and those on top will fall. Or maybe I just saw life this way.

I shove my hands deep in my coat pockets, pushing my fingers down hard, pretending that if I don't feel the cold I won't feel the loss.

I drive away from my street and end up parked in front of the church. I sat in this same church Sunday after Sunday, year after year, never tiring of seeing Christ on the cross, head hanging in agonizing glory, feet stacked and nailed, body bloody and skinny, beautiful in its sacrifice. The vision of the man on the cross is endlessly new and endlessly unchanging. Even as a boy – maybe especially as a boy – I understood that I was supposed to feel the sadness and promise of the moment on the cross. I felt the sadness. For years I assumed that in time I would come to believe in the other half of the crucifixion. Although my mother's belief resided deep in her marrow, I realized I could only dream of one day believing.

I believed in every moment up to and including Good Friday. I had no trouble believing that a guy named Jesus suffered and died on a hill some two thousand years ago, killed by people who feared and hated the man he claimed to be.

Sitting in church with my siblings, my mother, and sometimes my father, I would lose myself in the language of the liturgy and the hesitant beauty of the heartfelt hymns. But the rituals always failed to hold me completely. As I got older I began looking around: at the crucifix, the priest, the altar boys, the pretty girls, and the beautiful women. I was still young and frightened enough to feel sinful about wanting the entire female congregation. And by wanting them I meant . . . I didn't know what I meant. All I knew was that I sinned hundreds of times every Sunday morning. Thoughts were sins – I learned that early. Just wanting to touch a woman was the same thing as actually touching her! It was clearly a lose-lose situation. Not only did I sin, I didn't even get to touch. Watching the girls and women parade to and from Holy Communion was nearly unbearable.

While we all had our favorites, most of us – my best friend Rick and I in particular – practically held our breath while awaiting the contrite Cathy S. Along with her gorgeous girl-next-door face and cinder-black hair, Cathy had a kind word for everyone, including harmless thugs like us.

Cathy had a sister whose mind and body had been crippled by a disease whose name none of us took the time or effort to discover. I never even knew her first name, although to this day I can tell you the names of Cathy's two brothers. We watched each Sunday as a member of Cathy's family, sometimes Cathy herself, pushed the crippled (the "disabled" did not yet exist), nameless girl in her wheelchair up to the Communion rail, her body leaning over the chair's metal railing as if she and her chair rotated on the axis of a harsher earth.

For me at least, Cathy's beauty was a divine distraction. Not only did she distract me from the palpable boredom of the service, but she also carried me away from her sister and the unseen millions like her. I didn't have to cry for the wheelchair-bound girl; I didn't have to hide my discomfort by defensive mockery or suppressed snickering. I never had to confront the paradox of the parallel existences I witnessed: the crippled girl here, condemned to an early death, her beautiful sister there. I needed only to gawk at Cathy and mutter misunderstood words about her body and mine, words whose meanings I would know nothing about for many years to come.

Cathy's sister, her name still just one more mystery, has been dead for nearly a quarter of a century. Where Cathy is now I do not know. I'm sure she's still lovely. I hope she has married a man who cares enough to learn the names of handicapped children in wheelchairs.

As I got older, my attendance at Mass didn't so much end as dissolve. A few of my friends and I church-dated with girlfriends for a while. Others began staying home under the twin avalanches of hangovers and doubt, joking that their church of choice was St. Skepticism.

Growing up in the church, I carried a terrible secret: every Sunday morning, as I sat in church with my family, with friends, or alone with my doubt, I fought an image. In the image – it's the same every time – a man walks into the nave, ignoring the bowls of holy water, where he should be dipping the tips of his fingers and making the sign of the cross. He neglects to genuflect. As the congregation kneels, sits, and stands in keeping with the cadence of the ritual, the stranger raises a gun and fires several bullets into the chest of the priest, who falls dead on the altar. Screams erupt from the congregation. I imagine this happening during the Offertory, just as the priest elevates the host above his head and toward God. If not then, the shooting happens when the priest raises the chalice. The sound of the hand-held bells – rung by the eponymous altar boy – will be linked forever with the shots and the death and the priest and the aborted Offertory. Other times the priest is shot when removing the consecrated hosts from the tabernacle, his back to the congregation, his hands inside Christ's tiny cavern. Wine, water, and dead end, the other three altar boys, as well as bells, end up frightened but unharmed.

After years of distance and reflection, I can say honestly that I never wanted a priest, or anybody else, to be shot. I hated and feared violence then as I hate and fear it now. I would get nauseated watching other boys fight. The image entered the church and my mind as regularly and as unobtrusively as a fly in summer. As I grew up, I convinced myself these senseless, violent images could be blamed on the violent films we sneaked into the drive-in to watch, or on the police shows I watched while naively and ignorantly perched behind a wobbly TV tray on Saturday afternoons. I believe now that the images came from nothing more than the priest's utter vulnerability. One more sacrificial lamb. In confession I tried to confess the sin of this recurring image, but I was always afraid to say the words, so I never did. At eight and ten and twelve years old I just figured I would die with this sin on my soul.

From age ten or so until I entered an all-boy Catholic high school, I served Mass as an altar boy. I loved going into the church before anybody else, preparing the altar for the priest. There were candles to light and cruets to fill. On Sundays, holy days, weddings, and funerals, it took four altar boys to perform the duties of our office. We'd walk into the church, put on our black cassocks and white surplices, then set up.

I loved serving when Father Tift presided over the Mass. Thomas Tift was a short man with a slight lisp and an explosive laugh. He walked around the church and through the halls of the school with a smile on his face. He knew everybody's name – and I mean everybody's. I doubt there was a single kid from kindergarten through the eighth grade whom Father Tift did not acknowledge by name. He'd remember what sport you played or what club you were in. He talked to me as if I were the only person alive. When I think of the horrors heaped upon altar boys and other Catholic children by perverted priests, I'm happy I fled the church when I did. But then I remember Father Tift, the quintessential priest: good, kind, caring, smart, curious, devout, hopeful, joyous.

I saw him angry only once. There was talk of a party at an eighth-grader's house when the kid's parents were out of town. The host's high-school brother or sister would be in charge, which we all knew was a joke. There would be alcohol. All the cool kids were going. I was clearly not one of the cool kids, but my sense of humor and willingness to get in trouble for a laugh had won me a place in the bullpen of cool. The more whispers there were about the party, the more it grew in our imaginations: all the popular girls, alcohol, missing parents. Although I begged my parents to let me go, my mother wouldn't have it. She never gave reasons for any denied request. "Because I said so" was about as much as I ever got from her. For her the word "party" was undoubtedly a synonym for sin. All my dad needed to hear was her no, and no it was. The Monday after the party, I saw Father Tift walking to the school office like a man possessed. I hoped he was angry with Sister Concepta or Sister Gerald, the two main scourges of my grade-school years. He walked fast, had a scowl on his face, and didn't seem to notice anybody or anything. Somehow he'd gotten wind of the party. He put together a list of as many partygoers as he could and began calling parents. When he saw me a few days later, after he'd calmed down some, he told me how glad he was to hear I hadn't attended. He was proud of me. I accepted his praise like the hypocrite I was and am, but I was ashamed that I had wanted to go so badly, and for all the wrong reasons. Because my mother hadn't given me any reason for withholding her permission, I gave her none of the credit for Father Tift's pride in my not going. Perhaps she had a sixth sense about these things. I'll never know.

The other priests of my youth included Father Theodore Blair, a good man, the founding pastor of St. Bees. He mumbled his way through Mass, never befriending us altar boys but never treating us poorly either. He seemed forever lost in the clouds of heaven or in his multiple duties here on earth.

For a brief time we had Father James Sheil, fresh from Vietnam and with an attitude. Although I loved his five-minute sermons (let's get out of here before the napalm flies), he never took the time to learn our names. He was always in a hurry. God knows how many of the dead and dying he prayed over in the war, but he was not cut out for a safe suburban parish. He once locked my dad out of church as he approached the doors a few minutes late – he was coming from work and had hurried to meet us. My father didn't need much to keep him out of church; I think it was only love for my mom that kept him in. (He nearly left the church several times. One occasion came when he asked for extra time to pay the hefty tuition for his four children to attend St. Bees. A church official told him that perhaps he shouldn't have had so many kids. Neither my father nor the priest mentioned the church's ban on birth control.) Father Sheil left in the same smoky hurry he arrived in.

Then there was Father Robert Friedel, a prick of a priest. He screamed at us for the slightest infraction. Nobody I knew liked the man. He knew none of us, nor did he seem to care. He wore his faith like leprosy.

By the time my mother got sick with cancer in my sophomore year of college, Father Tift was gone, Father Blair had retired, and I attended church only when my mother asked me to. By this time a drone named Father Bayer was pastor. For all his mumbling and neglect, Father Blair cared about his church and its people, a feeling I never got from his successor. One of his underlings was Father Thomas Cleaton. Although only in his early thirties at the time, the man seemed ancient. He had black hair, confirming his relative youth, but he seemed aged from carrying the burden of his faith and the duties of his office, as if they weighed as much as the brick building he worshipped in. He visited my mom as she lay dying. To my eyes his visits never appeared to offer her any solace, and he was always out of the house as quickly as possible.

The moments following the priest's final words, "The Mass is ended; go in peace," were my all-time favorite altar boy moments. I was alone with the symbols and the mysteries, especially the tabernacle, which reminded me of my grandfather and the hole in his throat.

As a boy I spent hours staring at the curtain that covered my grandfather's throat. The curtain did not blow, it only covered. No slight summer breezes lifted its cottony hem. It pushed out only from the man's breath, the heft of flesh in midsigh, or the clearing of the carved-up throat. Behind the curtain was a hole, rimmed with a dark red circle like a bruise. When he was seventy years old, my maternal grandfather, Cosimo Leo Gervasi, had his cancerous larynx removed. The operation and his hearty stock allowed him another twenty-two years of life. I was four when he had the operation, so I can't recall any voice from him except a heavy Italian accent engulfed in a raspy gasp. Although I knew the extra opening was simply the result of an operation, when I was a boy I wanted nothing more from my grandfather than to see inside that hole, which, because of Cosimo's storied and dangerous past, seemed more like a passageway than a scar from a lifesaving operation.

Twenty-two years before he would flee New York City to save his life, Cosimo left the Reggio di Calabria section of southern Italy. He never told anybody why he left the land of his birth.

Whatever his reasons for leaving – and there had to have been many, at least one having to do with the dream of a paradise across the ocean – in 1904, as a boy of twelve, he boarded a ship for the United States, carrying only clothes in a sack and a hunk of cheese for the ride over. Whether he cried for his family, longed for America, or both, I don't know. I do know that an uncle was to meet him at Ellis Island, but the family didn't get the uncle's letter until Cosimo had pushed off for America, sleeping at the bottom of the ship with his makeshift suitcase for a pillow. The letter stated that, regrettably, the uncle planned on returning to Italy immediately, which left Cosimo trapped alone in the New World with only his native tongue.

The story is that Cosimo spotted a beautiful girl with long red hair. Irish and Italian immigrants either loved or hated each other. In this case it was love. My grandma, Anna Donahue, seventeen years old and nearly 100 percent Irish, married the twenty-year-old Cosimo in 1912. Anna's parents hated Cosimo for being Italian and for falling in love with their daughter. They did not attend the wedding. Later that night my grandmother huddled with her mother under a streetlight to show her the marriage license.

Despite the heartache it surely caused my grandmother, whose heart was big enough to make Mother Teresa seem like a two-bit street hustler, I fell in love with this moment as I imagined the scene. I can see the mother and her daughter, huddled against the cold, reading the words "Anna," "Cosimo," and "marriage" by the glow of gaslight, the daughter frightened but ecstatic, the mother worried but secretly happy that perhaps her daughter had found the love all the talk was about.

Cosimo worked at a series of jobs, some he talked about and others he didn't.

My family never said why, in late 1926 or 1927, Cosimo left New

York in the middle of the night without telling his wife or four children where or why he was going and if or when he would be back. He simply disappeared.

To discover the truth at the core of my history, I've had to burrow down through the layers of family myth.

Like most immigrants at the time, Cosimo gravitated toward his own people, and he soon had a job cleaning out spittoons at a nightclub on Coney Island. In Brooklyn he met his best friend, Frankie Yale, who went on to be ranked by the *World Telegram* as "No. 1 among Brooklyn's racketeers for a few tortured years." Only two of Yale's employees are of any interest to me. One is my grandfather, and the other is a young roughneck named Al Capone.

Yale had legitimate businesses. He owned a funeral home and sold his own brand of cigars called the Frank Yale Cigar. The boxes bore his mug. The cigars cost pennies, and soon "Frank Yale" became the way to describe any rotten-tasting stogie.

Along with these legitimate businesses, Yale had been supervising the Long Island shin of Capone's bootleg business, while Scarface ran the Chicago operation. The way the story goes, Yale began hijacking the booze and keeping the money for himself, or maybe Capone just thought that was going on, which in those days with those men amounted to the same thing. There was also talk of a grudge between the two old friends over Capone's suspicion that Yale was involved in the murder of Al's pal James "Filesey" De Amato. It was De Amato who told Capone that Yale was hijacking the booze.

Whatever the case, on Sunday, July 1, 1928, while he was driving his new Lincoln along 44th Street in the Borough Park section of Brooklyn, Yale died in a flurry of Capone-ordered bullets. Nobody has to imagine the scene, since it's been played out countless times on television and in the movies. Different men, similar reasons, same results. According to a story in the *World Telegram* from 1950, the cops covered Yale's bloody body with a blanket "when they found Yale dead . . . but one hand stuck out, and the late afternoon sun shone dazzlingly on the [four-carat diamond] ring Capone had given him." Families and nations have their myths.

Yale's funeral was a lavish affair:

> On July 5 Yale had his grand funeral, the likes of which New York had never seen. Two hundred automobiles filled with mourners followed the coffin through hushed Brooklyn streets lined with thousands of spectators. There were 38 cars filled with floral tributes. One of them, in the first car, was a huge 15-foot-high "F.Y." in pink roses and white lilies. . . . More than 15,000 persons crowded around the church where funeral services were held. And Frankie Yale had a police escort on his last ride – 10 motorcycle cops and many more afoot. It was grand.

The *Brooklyn Eagle* described another of Yale's floral arrangements as being "easily 20 feet high on which a heart of white roses was punctured by a violet and white dagger and from which red roses dripped to make a bleeding heart." After his requiem High Mass at the Church of St. Rosalie, where he lay in his coffin with a rosary entwined in his fingers, Yale was laid to rest at Holy Cross Cemetery.

Like Capone, Yale was certainly no angel and deserves no tears. He was nicknamed "the Executioner," and it is said that he would walk up to an enemy, press his gun against the unfortunate's head, and fire. To pave the way for Capone's ascendancy in Chicago, Yale is believed to have murdered Big Jim Colosimo in 1920 and Dion O'Bannion four years later. Although police could never prove Yale's guilt, they were convinced he committed the murders. Yale had been in Chicago "visiting" on the dates when Colosimo and O'Bannion were killed. These killings opened the door to crime ownership in Chicago for the two transplanted New Yorkers, Al Capone and Johnny Torrio.

Although he was arrested numerous times from age nineteen until his death at thirty-five, including being charged with two murders, Yale was convicted only on minor charges.

But my grandmother and history differ in their stories of Yale, whom the *New York Daily News* described as a "beefy-faced bully with slicked hair, small ears, a big nose and an even bigger ego." Because Yale, also known as the Baron of Bath Beach, took an ocean-orphaned Italian immigrant child under his tainted wing, my grandmother considered him an ally in her war against the changes of a new century and a new country. She knew nothing of his reputation or his business, we were told; she understood only that he helped a twelve-year-old boy who was to become her husband and my grandfather.

We were always given the impression that Yale was an older man, a surrogate father and mentor to my grandfather. But Yale was in fact a year younger than my grandfather. He was also godfather to one of my uncles.

My grandmother told about cooking spaghetti for Yale and his leaving fifty dollars under his plate after wiping it clean with the crust of his bread. Once, when my grandfather was in the hospital after he "accidentally shot himself in the leg," Yale came to give her money. She said, "Frankie, no," but she needed the money and so she took it. Yale's generosity was not confined to my grandmother. He had a reputation for helping the poor of his neighborhood, and he gave thousands of dollars to his parish. "He gave [the poor] money, clothes and food baskets at holiday time and fixed little legal matters for their erring young." During a coal shortage in the early twenties, Yale got hold of a heap of the black gold and spread it around the neighborhood.

Yale had survived two previous attempts on his life. One occurred in 1925 as he drove home from a Coney Island speakeasy. My grandparents were at the same club that night. My aunts tell the story that Yale asked my grandfather to drive his wife home, but my grandfather begged off for some reason that Yale accepted. A year to the day before Yale's murder, somebody had tried to kill him but had missed.

Whether my grandfather knew of Yale's hijacking and wanted no part of it or was a part of it and wanted out, I don't know. Perhaps he was frightened by the early attempts on Yale's life. I do know that my grandfather made almost twenty thousand dollars running booze in New York and lost it all in the Depression. I also don't know whether he was more afraid of Yale or Capone, or if he just woke up one day in a situation he never imagined being in, realizing he had crossed a line he never really saw. Whatever the case, he left New York in the middle of the night without a word to my grandmother about where he was going or when she'd hear from him. She and her four children lived in New York until he sent for them from his new home in Cleveland.

My grandfather lived the rest of his life in greater Cleveland. He did not leave the state from 1926 until his death in 1984. My grandmother stayed put as well; she died there in 1992 at the age of ninety-six. After years of working as a milkman and at a bakery, Cosimo was let go just days short of being eligible for a pension. A blue-collar tenet was born that day: never trust a big company or the Republican Party. They're no friends of the workingman.

Cosimo lived to bury his baby daughter Edith, dead from pneumonia at one year old, and his youngest daughter, Christine – my mother. He would cry for Christine from her death in 1979 until his in 1984.

Aside from the hole in his throat and his love for me, what I remember most is my grandfather's pride in his rose garden, something he worked on every year until he was too old to walk without help. Whenever I had finished cutting his grass, he would insist that I wash up, sprinkle powder on my torso, and change into one of his crisp, clean "Italian" T-shirts, now crudely called "wife beaters."

Even my grandmother admitted that my grandfather hit her – once. She told him that if he ever did it again, she would leave him. Whether it was this threat, or love, or shame, my grandma swore he never hit her again. She went to her grave at ninety-six, after birthing eight children, believing herself to be a woman of dignity (which she was) because my grandfather had never seen her naked in their seventy-two years as a married couple.

Cosimo was a loving, though not demonstrative, grandfather. He was adored by his four daughters and often despised by his three sons, who found him tough, demanding, and unforgiving. Though my grandfather was only five foot six in shoes and weighed no more than 140 pounds, his sons feared him. For the rest of their lives, I would hear my uncles – men in their fifties, sixties, and seventies – still complaining that their father never told them he loved them. It is a parent's curse for a child to need something that you cannot or will not give.

My grandfather wore his curtain the way Errol Flynn might have worn an ascot. The tiny cotton curtain, about the size of a deck of cards, was attached by two strings on the bottom and two on top, keeping my grandfather safe from airborne contaminants, not to mention flying and crawling insects.

Although I convinced myself I wanted to see inside my grandfather's throat, it was far more interesting when the hole was covered. The closed curtain promised a drama. As much as I love the theater, I'm still most excited in those few slow seconds when the curtain rises or parts. At those moments anything is possible. In those moments the story is still mine to imagine or to create.

I felt this same way about the altar tabernacle. Sitting in church, I would focus on the tabernacle as a way of ignoring the crucifix, afraid of what images would assault me. The tabernacle was the tomb before the stone was rolled away. To imagine what was inside became to me one of the greatest wonders of this strange religion.

In my final days of serving as an altar boy, one day when the priest was called back to the sacristy by another priest or deacon, I saw that he had left the tabernacle open and unlocked. All that separated me from this sanctum sanctorum were my own lack of guts and a short, heavy velvet curtain. I had watched numerous times as the priest's hands passed through the drapes and then returned safely with the golden bowl full of hosts. Surely I had nothing to fear.

Conquering my lack of guts, temporarily eclipsed by curiosity, or hunger for beholding a mystery, or wanting something to see and touch to validate my tenuous faith, I walked up the altar steps, grateful for the quieting carpet, and looked around again to make sure I was alone. I grabbed the candle snuffer as a prop in case I was caught, although the smoke from the extinguished candles had wafted up and away minutes before. The priest's voice still boomed safely from the sacristy. Taking the final step to the tabernacle, I practically lunged for the curtains. When I parted them, I saw it all. The beautiful gold tabernacle was an empty box. As empty as it was beautiful, as beautiful as it was empty. I turned away. I knew the consecrated hosts were with the priest, but even if they had not been, I had expected far more. I suppose I wanted some kind of light, or a tiny, magnificent drama, or the Virgin mother's smile, or the hand of God, or a message I could read in times of doubt, or some secret revealed in some way, but all I could feel was utter disappointment. There was nothing there. It could have been a mailbox. I longed to return to the other side of the velvet drapes cloaking the small monument in monumental mystery.

My grandfather's throat was as sacred as the tabernacle. It led to places and promises. I imagined the drama being acted behind his closed curtain. I could see my grandfather's past, being with him in Italy as a twelve-year-old, kissing his mother good-bye, never to see her again, never to see his father and brothers and sisters, wiping the tears from his face with his tattered shirt sleeve, because surely he cried – my God, how could he not – walking up the wobbly gangway to the ship that would carry him across the Atlantic Ocean to America, where while living in New York City he would one day catch a streak of red out of the corner of his eye, and that streak of red would be a lock of hair on a pretty seventeen-year-old Brooklyn girl from a troubled family, and the two would marry and have children and then the new American would find himself in trouble with gangsters and have to flee New York City in the middle of the night without his family's knowing where he had gone, "I'll send for you" the only promise. And he did, when he got to Cleveland, where more children came, eight in all until Baby Edith, as she would be known forever, died of pneumonia the same week the man would lose his job, and then one more baby would be born, Christine, and she would live down the street from a boy she would not know until the two were in their early twenties, and then the boy would go to the Korean War, and three years after he came back they'd be married, and a year later their son would be born, and he wouldn't talk for the first four years of his life, and then the couple would move to Parma, Ohio, where fifteen years after the move, the woman would develop breast cancer and be dead at forty-four, and the boy who didn't talk for the first four years of his life would, at forty-four, be pulled back to these people who first came to him as mysteries, as something passing up and through the tabernacle throat of a grandfather at whose feet the boy sat.

A photograph in the twenty-fifth anniversary edition of the St. Bridget's yearbook, which I picked up from a friend not long ago, shows an unidentified woman standing alone in a field where brown bushes and weeds stick up through the swampland now covered in snow. The sign reads, "Future home of St. Bridget's Church." I'm touched by the woman in the picture, who reminds me of my mother. Standing as tall as the sign, the woman is bundled up in a long heavy coat. Her head is wrapped in a scarf, and her gloved hands hold on to the signpost nearest her. It's the way she's holding on to the sign that touches me – precisely the way a woman would hold the arm of a man she loved walking with, being with, who made her feel safe and comfortable and loved. She appears to know that this church, promised in the winter of 1956, will be no ordinary church.

The diocese bought twelve acres on which Father Theodore J. Blair would build a church and a school, creating a brick-bound house of memories for a boy whose sensibilities and imagination they shaped.

Always the seekers and finders of symbols, the Catholics of this future parish held the groundbreaking ceremony on December 8, the Feast of the Immaculate Conception, standing in the rain, holding umbrellas, praying for a blessed beginning as their chilled breath showed itself before disappearing into time. In another photograph Father Blair stands out front without an umbrella, looking very much at peace, his hands folded in front of him as he stares straight out at the camera, or at God, or at the future of a church and its people.

The Sisters of Saint Joseph ruled the classrooms of St. Bridget's. The first Mass was offered on February 1, 1959, the feast of St. Bridget, a sixth-century Irish woman said to be of extreme beauty and piety. Her father, of royal blood, attempted to give his beautiful daughter in marriage, but Bridget refused. We were taught that Bridget's mother was a slave, and it was that slave blood that helped this young woman rise up against her father and become a nun.

A statue of the beautiful woman from Ireland used to stand sentry on the choir loft of the church, watching over us as we played in the parking lot and fields where we did our growing.

Six months after my mother's death, a fire broke out in the church on Saturday afternoon, June 30, gutting the interior and destroying just-purchased stained-glass windows.

As I entered my early teens as an altar boy, the easy access to wine became more than I and a few of my colleagues could resist. We were often asked to do chores around the church. One year during Lent, my friend TC and I were moving furniture or cleaning the floors or rearranging cassocks and surplices in the sacristy when we happened upon the wine. Bottles and bottles of it. Too many for a bottle or two to be missed, we decided. And so we began drinking. We were careful. We'd each take a drink and then hide the bottle behind a row of full ones, never leaving it out. After a few gulps, we got hungry. Boxes of unconsecrated hosts were stacked high above us on top of a large chest of drawers. With me keeping watch, TC climbed up on the chest and lowered a box to me. We opened it and marveled at the sheer number of hosts tied tight in plastic bags. A relative harvest of hosts. We each grabbed a handful and returned the box to its shelf. The hosts were bland, of course, but we discovered they tasted better if we stacked two or three together and ate them at the same time. Soon we began dunking them in wine, and we were having ourselves quite a feast. I was a little surprised to see that the box of hosts came from someplace like Milwaukee. Although I had convinced myself I understood the concepts of consecration and transubstantiation, I just could not get my mind around the idea that some factory in Milwaukee pumped out the body of Christ the way factories churned out car parts or sugary cereals.

Not long into our drinking and snacking, I was overcome by guilt and suggested we at least practice our roles in the Passion play, to be performed on the upcoming Palm Sunday. Right after the part of the Passion where Pilate offers the crowd a choice of releasing Jesus or the murderer Barabbas, TC and I played our parts to the hilt, with me acting as the objective narrator, Pilate, and also as a member of the crowd:

"You brought this man to me and accused him of inciting the people to revolt. I have conducted my investigation in your presence and have not found this man guilty of the charges you have brought against him, nor did Herod, for he sent him back to us. So no capital crime has been committed by him. Therefore I shall have him flogged and then release him."

But all together they shouted, and we shouted along with them,

"Away with this man! Release Barabbas to us." Again Pilate addressed them, still wishing to release Jesus, but they continued their shouting, "Crucify him! Crucify him!"

We took a break to grab a few more hosts and pass the bottle back and forth, wiping our chins like revelers in a frontier saloon:

Pilate addressed them for the third time, "What evil has this man done? I found him guilty of no capital crime. Therefore I shall have him flogged and then release him." With loud shouts, however, they persisted in calling for his crucifixion, and their voices prevailed. The verdict of Pilate was that their demand should be granted. So he released the man who had been imprisoned for rebellion and murder, for whom they asked, and he handed Jesus over to them to deal with as they wished.

And then, without the crowd shouting along with us, TC and I continued drinking wine and eating hosts and shouting as loudly as if we were in the stands of a football game, "Give us Barabbas. Give us Barabbas. Crucify him. Crucify him. Crucify him."

Although part of this was harmless playacting by two pubescent boys high on flying hormones and cheap wine, for me, at least, it was something more. I was beginning to pierce the surface of my religion, to see through curtains, to learn what was behind doors I had been forbidden, or had forbidden myself, to open. I had stolen wine from the church and drunk it before it had the chance to become Christ's blood, as if the blood of Christ were anything other than cheap wine. I had eaten Christ's body when it was nothing more than bland, flat crackers from Milwaukee. It was nothing more than bland, flat crackers from Milwaukee. It was as though once I learned the source of the body and blood, I could no longer buy the lie of transubstantiation. I felt a unity that day with the crowd calling out to Pilate.

Although I doubt if I understood, except perhaps on the most visceral level, that this was going on, I do know my pulling away from faith was given a good yank that day. But I was still stitched pretty tightly into the fabric of my faith because of what happened on the way home.

TC and I had finished a whole bottle of wine and a solid stack of hosts. We crammed the partially eaten packet into the bottom of the box, and TC shoved the empty bottle under his coat. We checked for any evidence of our theft and debauchery, and when we were satisfied, we left the sacristy, leaving no signs behind except perhaps the vestiges of sound waves calling for the death of our Lord. When TC split off to use the shortcut to his house, he smashed the empty wine bottle against the curb and whooped in victory. I began to feel sick. We had undoubtedly drunk the wine too fast and too foolishly, and the crackers probably did my digestive system no good either. Suddenly I was sick and frightened for other reasons. Ringing in my ears was my own voice, screaming out gleefully for a crucifixion. And then another voice joined my own. In my drunken state I thought I recalled a nun's saying that if somebody sinned, the part of the body he sinned with could fall off. Or was it that wantonly eating and drinking consecrated hosts and blessed wine would cost the sinner dearly? Perhaps the priest had already blessed the hosts and the wine – a bulk blessing. I imagined my tongue falling out, my voice box being regurgitated, as I threw up the wine and hosts into the gray snow. Soon I expected my hands to leave my wrists and tumble dumbly to the lawns I ran through. I hoped to hell I had not inadvertently touched myself "down there" while we drank! What would I tell my parents when their eldest son arrived home minus a tongue, voice box, and hands? I would have to confess my sins of theft, drunkenness, drinking the blood of Christ and eating his flesh, wantonly and without regard. Not to mention my blasphemy.

I pushed through the gate of the fence that boxed in our backyard, feeling the freezing metal on my sinful, gloveless hands. When I got inside I dropped my coat, kicked off my boots at the landing, and went directly to my room, saying I was tired after working so hard, avoiding my mother's curiosity about my "helping out at the church."

When I awoke some hours later, feeling better, I looked down at my hands, still firmly attached to the rest of my body. My first thought was that I had gotten away with some major sinning, that we had not been caught by the priests, or worse, the nuns, that my parents suspected nothing, thinking their son was just tired after dutifully helping out the clergy at St. Bees.

But then I felt regret.

What a sign it would have been! This could have been my personal version of Thomas's wounds. I could have poked my fingers into the sides of my faith. I could have received a sign that faith was not a scantily clad myth, a simply complex story. At that moment, I would have traded my hands for knowing for sure that there was somebody to sin against, my larynx for somebody to blaspheme, my tongue for somebody's holy flesh to eat, my entire mouth for somebody's holy blood to drink.

4

I manage to stay away from the old neighborhood until late July, but in my memory it's almost always winter here. It's impossible not to recall the winters of 1978 and '79, when despair hovered over my home the way the record snows covered the streets, sidewalks, and lawns.

People still talk about those winters, blizzards with eighty-mile-an-hour winds and perpetual snow, heavy and layered, tainted with dog piss and exhaust fumes, laden with portent. Headlines across the Midwest proclaimed those blizzards the century's worst. Ohio existed in a whiteout. The state was on hold. One blizzard of that winter killed a hundred people, some buried in snowdrifts. Thousands of people were stranded on roads and highways and in emergency shelters. The entire Ohio Turnpike was closed for the first time in forty-seven years. Three hundred soldiers descended on the state. Times were changing, and it seemed the elements knew what momentous times these were. After all, some teenager's mother was dying from breast cancer.

I was still foolish or romantic enough to believe that the storied winters were symbols in the unfolding myth of my life. The storms meant that something had indeed changed in the earth's atmosphere, at least the splinter of the earth known as Fairlawn Drive. Not only was a young woman dying, but weather patterns seemed to echo this death, granting it the gravitas it certainly warranted.

I remember one night not long before my mother died. My father, brother, two sisters, and I were driving home from visiting my mother in the hospital. The roads seemed made of snow and ice: last week's snow covered by the other day's freezing rain, slicked by this morning's fresh fall, stapled with the city's salt. Morose and angry, I sat stiff and silent in the car. I don't remember what we said to each other. If there was talk, it no doubt covered the familiar ground of a family in crisis. Families losing one of their own are trained to look for the tiniest prospect of hope. "I think this new medicine is helping the swelling." "That doctor seemed to really care. Maybe she knows something other doctors haven't thought of yet." "Did the doctor say 'could' or 'would'?" "She doesn't seem to be in as much pain." "Perhaps she won't scream in the middle of the night."

Our woe metastasized as we drove home in the heavy snow. In the midst of the silence or of the family's posthospital myth-making, my father noticed a hitchhiker standing out in the road. With all lane lines and curbs buried in winter, my dad began to ease the car toward the hitchhiking kid. I wondered what he was doing. Changing lanes in this weather took a concentration and caution I wasn't sure a man in deep grief possessed. Slowly we made our way closer to the hitchhiker on the side of the street, our car pushed and pulled by the snow and ice. We heard black-caked slush knocking the bottom of the car. All four of us kids decried my father's stopping for the hitchhiker. We couldn't believe it.

The kid was probably drunk or high, I remember thinking, likely because I spent most of the eighteen months of my mother's illness in one or both of these twin states of chemical distraction. My brother and sisters protested as well.

"Nobody should have to be out hitchhiking on a night like this," my father said. "It's not fit for anybody out here."

So we picked up the kid. He looked to be in his late teens. But I remember nothing of what he said, where he needed to go, or where we took him. He reeked of cigarettes. Only a few inches of his face showed through the layers of clothes. My dad talked with him, asking where he was going and why he was out on a night like this. He might even have lectured the kid on the dangers of hitch-hiking. Nobody else in the car said a word. It seemed as if he was with us for hours, but I'm sure it was only minutes.

Since then I've thought a lot about what my father meant by "on a night like this." More than likely he was merely referring to the weather, but I've always believed it was something more. Perhaps "a night like this" also meant a night preceding the quickly arriving day when a wife and mother would die. A night like the one where an eighteen-year-old wanted to be that kid hitchhiking in the storm, a member of some other family, a resident in a parallel universe called somebody else's life. I wonder if my father hoped for some kind of karma. Pick up a hitchhiker on a snowy night, have your wife for a few more weeks, days, hours.

Perhaps it was something more. Perhaps at that moment my father longed for the flesh-on-flesh human contact of two people in trouble, of strangers coming together to help one another. We gave the hitchhiker a ride in a blizzard-heavy winter. He helped us by reminding us that there is a world of people in need of one thing or another. In need of each other. I know my father could do nothing to save his wife, but he could reach across the field of a blizzard and help a stranger alone on a street. Whereas for me and my siblings grief combusted into anger, maybe for my dad it brought forth an inexplicable act of kindness.

We could never understand his actions of that night. My father had been a Cleveland homicide detective who warned us about the grim perils of picking up hitchhikers. We heard tales of good Samaritans being stabbed to death. I'll probably never know why he did it. I'm sure I've inflated this night's importance beyond all reason. It's over twenty-five years later, and the only thing my dad says about that night is that "it wasn't fit for man or beast out there," and then he quickly turns away.

45

But on this late July day the sun is shining, and I can practically see the summer heat bubbling up from the street. I park in the army reserve lot across from the Hauserman Road end of our street and walk past house after identical house. Fairlawn Drive is filled with the feelings and sounds of summer.

I recall one summer night when my friends and I climbed the fences surrounding the army reserve armory, fences that caged the army trucks. This was the same place we spent hours playing baseball and football. We always played baseball in the armory parking lot; the end of the pavement and later a row of pines served as our home-run fences. We played right alongside the jeeps and transport trucks. We understood the armory less as a meeting place for army reserves than as evidence of the government's reach. The older we got – with Vietnam marching on – the more we, or at least I, worried about having to go to war.

Our football field was a stretch of grass that ran alongside the armory parking lot. The field was long enough to allow for long passes and breakaway runs. Not one of us was much interested in school sports. What I remember most about that time is my white aluminum bat. It was the first aluminum bat in the neighborhood, and it loved the feel of the rubber-coated balls we used.

On this night we each told our parents we were sleeping in somebody else's backyard, a routine and always effective ploy. Once over the fences without being shot (or so we imagined; I doubt if a soul was around), we found a truck with a canvas top, which put us in mind of a covered wagon. Six of us started out, but only three lasted the night without fleeing. One feared army reprisals; another feared his parents' punishment; one said he just couldn't get to sleep. Those who retreated were taunted, the butt of invective and aspersions on their manhood. Most of the night we survivors told stories about waking up in Angola or Vietnam, ready to fight, kill, die. After a few hours of telling stories and eating chips, we went to sleep. I slept like a baby. But my tough act was a fraud; I knew where I stood on the thought of going to war. The Vietnam War seemed as if it would go on forever. My father, a Korean War veteran, assured me that if I were drafted he would personally drive me to the Canadian border. I loved him for this, yet I didn't completely understand his willingness to make a draft dodger out of his eldest son. It felt wrong and right, right and wrong.

Several weeks ago I found a picture of these boys, and I call it to mind as I walk. I want to reach into the photo and warn them, shake them awake and let them know what awaits them. We smile for the camera. Our hats and coats are sprinkled with snow, and more snow covers the lawns and roofs. Women are alive everywhere you look. I'm in a maroon winter jacket and blue knit hat. My cheeks and belly look full. I'm smiling. I stare at my face. Not a hint anywhere. Not a hint that in a few short years I'll be lost in the landfill of alcohol and drugs, having shed my faith. How could that boy need to escape this life? No sign at all that I would live without faith. One of the other boys in the photo, brown jacket zipped up tight, ski mask askew, probably nine in this photo, will be the neighborhood pot dealer by the time he's in the eighth grade. Another kid, the only one not smiling, has caught many of my passes on the football field. I can see him now, faking a short pattern and then going long. I lead him almost perfectly, around the tree. Although he doesn't have to jump, he wants to jump anyway, catching the ball with one hand and then pulling it to his chest as he enters the end zone. That hand – was it his right or left? – is still pure, still fifteen years away from striking his wife's pretty face.

I've studied the picture often, from various angles, looking at it through a magnifying glass, holding it under fluorescent lamps or up to the light of morning, clenching it in a fist, even looking at it through tears, and nothing in it tells a thing about the futures we'd make.

Lawnmowers cut through the day as I get farther from the armory. Kids on bikes scream to each other. One boy has taken a tumble. No problem; he picks up his bike and jumps back on. His two friends don't even slow down. They know it's nothing serious. They're kids, after all. And it's summer.

Staying away from Tom's end of the street is the focus of today's visit. Other people have lived and died here. Most of them went to work, raised their kids, took in movies, manicured their lawns.

Not five houses from where I walk is the place I met the new girl who moved onto our street. I can see her now, chasing a younger boy. The sun beams down on us all as one more promise of good fortune. Soon other boys help the new boy, perhaps as a way of welcoming him to the neighborhood and showing him the solidarity of their sex. We boys stick together in this neighborhood, buddy. But I'm a couple of years older, perhaps twelve. I've never known the "I hate girls" stage I hear I'm supposed to have experienced as a youngster. Love of a girl named Cheryl weakened me nearly to illness at age five. The summer I was seven, a cousin of a friend visited the neighborhood for a week. I can't recall her name, but when she went home, I threw myself on my bed and damned to hell all flora and fauna. I used to read about girls, buy the books they bought. (I remember *Strawberry Girl* in particular.) I wanted to learn their ways, get a glimpse inside their minds, find out what they liked – in life, in boys.

Sequestered from the outside world, the pubescent boys in my neighborhood had their visions of women and sex formed by fear and ignorance, the twin engines of boyhood. When it came to girls, my friends and I lived primarily in a state of ignorant awe.

Our ignorance knew no bounds. Some of the views that passed for knowledge were laughable.

I've forgotten who asked the first question. The talk went something like this:

"When is a girl a broad?"

"What are you, stupid?" we asked, as we always did. In our world there were no stupid answers, only stupid questions.

"It's just another word for slut," somebody else said.

"No it isn't."

"A girl is a broad when she's old enough to wear a bra," I said. "Broad, bra. Get it?" As the person trusted in all matters related to words, I actually got away with this pseudoetymology.

"I knew it was something like that," one of them said.

One day a few of us are standing around a corner mailbox after a pickup football game. It's fall, and the smell of burning leaves wafts off the ground. The sidewalk feels cold beneath our boots, and we wipe our noses on our sweatshirt sleeves.

I don't remember who asked the question that afternoon, but I remember the words he used.

"What happens if you take a leak when you're making love?"

"Are you stupid?" we all said.

"You'll never have to worry about it, man," I said.

"Yeah. You'll need to grow one first."

"No, really," the questioner said. "I'm serious. What do you do? I don't want to, you know, go inside her."

We all fell silent; searching eyes, faces, sidewalk, and sky for answers.

Finally Dan, the oldest of us by almost a year, broke the silence. We knew he would because he had an older brother.

"You guys are idiots. I can't believe you. You just make sure to go to the john before you do it."

Among thankful mutters for older brothers, we went back to our game.

And on it went.

But on this sun-bleached day with a new girl in the neighborhood, life and its mysteries are clear and true. The young boy has something his sister wants – a scarf or a handkerchief, memory tells me. He speeds away from her. She stuns me still. Still, she stuns me. Her shoulder-length golden hair catches the sun. No, her hair draws the sun to it. She screams his name, but the scream isn't harsh or crude; it's a mixture of determination and a hint of the plaintive. Soon I join the golden-haired girl in her attempt to rescue her scarf. The kid in the striped shirt throws it to the new boy in the black shorts who's being chased. Several kids, munchkins all, flee and hide, getting into something or somewhere, disappearing and re-appearing, retaining their interest in the game long after the girl and I have given up. We pant and pant, I more than she.

I'm panting still.

"Hi. I'm Joe."

"Hi. I'm Lisa."

"You're the ones that moved into the Drolls' house."

"We're over there." She points to the Drolls' old place.

"Sorry I couldn't catch that kid."

"He's my brother," she spits out beautifully.

"I live in the brick house," I point.

Silence.

"Well," I say.

"See you."

"See you."

She turns and walks away.

I hang around for a bit to watch her departure. Her face stays with me. I long for her to turn around so I can gaze at it again. That wide smile, diminutive nose, several perfectly placed freckles. She's thin but not gawky, tall but not too tall. All girl, but tough and smart. I've come to these conclusions about her toughness and intelligence in a matter of minutes, of course. Natives judge the immigrants in the neighborhood based on far less than wild chases and clipped conversations. She's beautiful, and she didn't run away from me. That's more than enough.

She moves up her driveway now. Please turn around, I think. Please, God, make her turn around. As if the hand of God has reached down on command and turned Lisa's chin to the right, she turns toward me. And then quickly back, so quickly that she misses my wave. But still, she turned back. When she's out of sight I run toward home. I'm the fastest kid in the neighborhood. I sprint past my house because I can't stop running. She has golden hair. She's tough. She's smart. She's nice. She talked to me. She turned around. It's as if the sun has charged my body. My legs and arms are on fire. I don't even stop at the end of my street, barely glancing both ways to check for oncoming traffic on Hauserman Road. I'm convinced I'm too much even for a truck bearing down at fifty miles an hour. I can deflect semis and station wagons alike. I'm invincible. I've met woman. Suddenly I'm in the armory, then the woods. Almost falling, I pound down the dirt trail leading into the park, not slowing down until I'm at the creek. I splash through the water, then turn around and splash back, falling on my back in the wide open expanse of field surrounded by trees whose leaves all hold their pieces of the sun, as my heart pounds as though it could never stop, as if this is the pitch of life, as if a boy's life has no chance of reaching this pitch until a girl with golden hair tells him her name and turns around, as if this is the eternal pitch, the frequency available to all dreamers and lovers, the height of living that must never be forgotten by years, neglected by memory, denied by adulthood, denounced by cynicism, polluted by irony, laughed at by intellect, worn away by experience.

My heart begins to slow, and I dwell on how Lisa and I teamed up, formed a partnership before any words were spoken. It was as if the partnership were out there, waiting for us, and all we had to do was show up. And I lie there on par with the understory the woods tell, blissfully ignorant of words like sentimentalism and nostalgia, still unaware but hopeful that Lisa and I would join together, kiss and be kissed, while "Maggie May" provides our soundtrack, as we stretch out on the middle of her lawn, holding hands under a huge pine tree and dreaming of love like fucking lunatics.

Taking one final glance at Lisa's house, which is now lived in by God knows who and I don't give a shit, I head back to my car.

Maybe my middle-aged life needs a little sentimentalism, or just plain unadulterated emotion. Save me from my own dark dross! For years I've nurtured suspicion and cultivated skepticism. *I felt then*, I want to scream. More than now, more than at any time since. What happened to me? Why must I always pierce feeling with intellect, optimism with cynicism, authenticity with irony, light thoughts with dark facts? I do not know. I want to know.

Looking at Lisa's house that day and remembering our first meeting, I had no idea of what this trip back in time had yet to teach me.

A few years after the days Lisa and I kissed and held hands under her pine tree as we maniacally gazed up into the incomprehensible sky, a new stranger came to our neighborhood. The stranger took up residence in a young man's brain. Lisa's dad died of a brain aneurysm at thirty-seven. And then Lisa's family moved.

And now, over thirty years later, as I'm about to leave Fairlawn Drive for the thirtieth time in the past year, I can see Lisa's father in a plaid short-sleeved shirt, standing in the driveway with his life stretching before him, seeing his future as a series of new beginnings, knowing he's giving his kids a chance at a better life than his, wondering about the personalities of his grandchildren to come while his seven kids chase each other around their new neighborhood.

He seemed old to me then. Hell, he was somebody's husband. Hell, he was a golden-haired dream girl's father.

I start my car and drive away, before Lisa's dad has a chance to turn around in his driveway and not look back.

5

Six months after my last summertime visit back home, I'm on my way to meet my old friends Rick Holland and Dave Rinella. They knew Tom well and should be able to help me. I knew rumors had been circulating that Tom died of a heart attack or liver cancer. I also knew everybody privately suspected drugs.

Rick and Dave also know, or knew, me pretty well. I'm not sure how much I'll admit to them. I don't want to say how I've been haunted by Tom lately. (I wonder if they too regard Tom as our personal augury.) I don't want to discuss the nights I'm kept awake by fear. I decide to say nothing about how I'm living a good life on the surface while underneath, where the real truth resides, there lately seethes an unhealthy, burgeoning bleakness.

We haven't seen each other in years. I did see Rick at his mom's funeral seven years ago, but before that it had been at least ten years. I haven't seen Dave in two decades.

Rick and I met during a pickup baseball game in the field behind our houses. It must have been a Sunday or we would have been playing in the armory parking lot as we always did on weekdays and Saturdays. On Sundays reservists were required to show up and do whatever the hell they did besides screw us out of our place to play ball.

Rick had just hit a grounder to me at third. I picked up the ball and whipped it to the guy playing first. But Rick got in the way as he tore for the base, and the ball slammed into the middle of his back. The thwack sounded nasty; I knew it must have hurt. I laughed. I don't know why, but I laughed. When Rick heard me laughing, he turned around and rushed at me, pissed and fast. When he was a couple of feet away, I raised my fists in front of me.

I like to think that at that minute I apologized or said it was an accident – which it was – or perhaps had a genuinely sorry look that showed I didn't mean to hit him and was as confused by my laughter as he was. But I can't remember a thing except this: Rick stopped cold, right in front of me. I did say I was sorry then. The other guys used this moment as an opportunity to call it quits. When we played baseball, games would go on for hours and hours. To end a game it usually took somebody's being called home, a fistfight, or a lost ball. Suddenly it was just the two of us standing there. We talked about the play. I explained that I'd laughed because it was such a bad throw, and never did I think it would hit him. I certainly didn't know he was hurt so badly. He said he came at me because he thought I was laughing at his pain. We talked for another minute or so, then one of us said, "You want to do something?" The other guy said, "Sure." We stayed best friends during our final years of grade school and through high school and college. We were in each other's weddings, and then the drift began, as it always does, as it always must.

We've agreed to meet at eight o'clock sharp on a Saturday morning in late January at a McDonald's a block or so from where we grew up. It's nearly a year since I stood in the cemetery taking my first step down into the dark vortex I've been swirling in for the past eleven months.

The temperature has been below freezing for nearly three weeks. It seems appropriate that the mercury can't rise in these first few weeks of a new year. It's as if the time I'm trying to reenter is being cryogenically preserved. Today is one of the coldest days yet, and we're getting together to scour the grounds of the old drive-in, the place we spent nearly every weekend night and a good many weekday afternoons for a year or two during our middle teens.

This McDonald's is where we engaged in drunken brawls. We

spent too many nights of our late teen years raiding this place after we'd killed enough beer to drown every man, woman, and child in China – a country, I should add, that few of us could have located on a map. One night several of us, me included, actually leaped over the counter and went after a couple of guys flipping burgers who'd been foolish or stupid enough to question our right to rage in their place of employment. Someone called the cops, and a couple of us, me excluded, got arrested.

As I walk in I notice a guy who looks like a biker standing at the counter. I make sure not to make eye contact in case he believes it's still Friday night. He's close to six feet tall and husky. With his goatee, he looks menacing. And then he smiles.

"Hey, dick," Dave says, leaving the counter and coming over to give me a hug. "You didn't know it was me, did you?"

"Yes I did," I lie.

Rick enters the side door, clean-shaven and heavy. With Rick, being overweight is a good thing. A skinny guy well into adulthood, Rick was constantly trying to bulk up through weight training and protein shakes. Rick and I worked out together, Rick trying to gain weight and muscle, me trying to lose weight and find muscle as we pumped iron and listened to Aerosmith's "Sweet Emotion."

Because I haven't seen these guys since America entered what Gail Sheehy calls the post–September 11 "new now," I'm curious how they're doing with a changed world. They both recount their September 11ths. I too tell my tale, as we must, like scouts who have entered some netherworld and returned to report on it. We share stories of the day as we sip coffee, safe and hot.

I have to admit I'm surprised I'm not hearing talk of "nuking the towel heads." In our teens, with all of us pounding down beers and looking for something to do, we'd cruise around Parma in my black 1966 vw Bug or somebody else's beat-up, rusted car. Whoever drove would begin to joke about playing a game with a dangerous and dubious – although innocent, always just joking around – point system. This being the no-end-in-sight Cold War, a run-over Commie would garner some drunk and lucky driver fifty points. We'd laugh through our beers about getting ten points for running into a black man, though that's not what we called him. But we were the good guys, we'd tell each other. Some people actually did this shit. We just joked about it.

What we shared with the hated Soviets was a party line.

But of course it was more than a game. Parma had been identified by the Department of Justice and by twenty-seven state and federal judges as one of the most white and racist cities of its size in the country. One past president of the Parma City Council said on the record that he didn't want any "Negroes in Parma."

The United States sued my hometown in the seventies for violating the Fair Housing Act. Ten years later, Parma was again found to be in violation of the act as it strove to propagate its image as an all-white city. The feds took over supervision of the suburb's housing policies. Soon there was an affirmative marketing program for minorities, and the city was required to provide nearly a million dollars in aid and loans to potential minority home buyers.

A city of nearly 100,000, Parma still has only approximately 1 percent black residents, most of them clustered in the city's federal low-income housing. As recently as 2002, Parma had to freeze its hiring of city employees until it could demonstrate compliance with a court-ordered plan to recruit minorities. This was a full twelve years after the NAACP sued the city for discrimination. At that time, of the over five hundred city employees, only two were African Americans: one was a police officer, the other a clerk. In 2002 the ninety-eight-member fire department included not one black or one female. Not until 2003 did the city hire its first black firefighter.

Racism was as much a part of the atmosphere of our neighborhood as the factory fires at night, the carbon monoxide at dawn, and the incense on church holidays.

In 1996 one new black resident of Parma looked out his picture window late one night and discovered a seven-foot cross burning on his front lawn. Two years later a nine-year-old girl was the first to spot a ten-foot cross on her scorched lawn, after her family had lived in Parma all of nine days. One of the families had just settled a discrimination lawsuit that allowed them to move into a home in perpetually white Parma. Both families moved out of the city.

Both crimes were committed by "normal," pubescent suburban boys. In one case the perpetrators, twelve and fourteen, lived only five houses away. A friend of theirs had hauled the cross over a few streets on his mountain bike. The youths said they had no issues with the color of their neighbors' skin and believed the whole incident was blown out of proportion.

Rick and Dave cannot understand why I'm digging around in the remains of our mutual friend, and I'm doing a poor job of explaining myself to them.

"At times I think I embody everything that went wrong with our neighborhood. I've been divorced; I've had trouble with booze and drugs," I say. "My mom was my age when she died."

"So?" Dave says.

"What do you want to know?" Rick asks.

Already I'm in trouble. I'm not sure I can say what I want to derive from learning more about Tom and his death. I want his life to have mattered. I want the small incidents of our childhood to have mattered. I want to understand something more about life, about being alive. I want to let them know that I feel as if I've lost something of my self and that this is the only place it can possibly be because I've searched everywhere else I can imagine and have come up empty.

I have to be careful. Scaring them off is not what I want to do. We didn't grow up talking about dying by pieces. At some level I'm sure we're all relieved it was Tom dead at thirty-seven and not ourselves.

I try something different.

"I want to figure out how it all happened. How did Tom die at thirty-seven without anybody's really caring or feeling too surprised? How come so many of us have had trouble with alcohol and drugs? How come nearly every one of us has heard horror stories about somebody we used to hang with? Is it just us, or is this how most working-class kids our age behaved?"

My old friends don't answer. They sip their coffee as if I haven't said a word. Maybe it's just me.

I have a good life. Better than I could have expected. Better than most people I grew up with ever imagined. I have a great wife and kids. I have rewarding work as an English professor, writer, and editor. I have time for the things and people I love. If a good man is nothing more than one who does no harm, then I'm a good man. If a good man means too much more – and of course it does; most of the time I believe that of course it does – then I'm not. But I need to discover what I've left behind and what will never leave me.

How much of our pasts, those forgotten moments, faded images, lives on in the boys and girls of our youth, these men and women who peopled our pasts and then disappeared into them? At times it's as simple as a childhood friend's remembering something you do not; other times it is as confusing and complicated as a dead friend who seems to be pulling you back to your roots to discover where or why things went wrong.

The pull of the past has been getting incrementally worse. For months I've been waking up in the middle of the night and spending hours fighting off thoughts of death and hopelessness. I try to take a piss and get back to sleep before fear descends like an iron vulture. I'm frightened for my family, for myself, for my country – my God, our country – for all of us. And then I'll think of Tom, and I know I'll be awake all night.

Please help me, I want to say.

I say none of this, but I've said too much.

We sip our coffee.

"Did you drink last night?" Rick asks Dave.

"No. I thought about it, but I knew I'd be getting up early to be here, and I didn't want to sleep in."

Talk of drinking suddenly sounds good. How I would love to once again lose myself in alcohol, just for a while, long enough to get through whatever's been plaguing me.

"Tom was a good guy," Rick says. "He was just fucked up."

Although I come close a couple of times, I don't tell these old friends how I've been haunted lately. I don't say anything about the fear that keeps me awake or about the recent emptiness. I'm afraid to admit to these demons.

A few months after my mom died, another friend and I were sitting in my car smoking pot. I began talking about how it was to lose my mother, how I felt guilty at being glad about the little things I wasn't going to have to do anymore. I wouldn't have to give her morphine shots; there wouldn't be medicine all over the house; no more worry about bad days. We no longer had to face the prospect of her dying, just the reality of her death. And . . .

"I have to get going," my friend said.

We could talk for hours about sports or school or music or parties or girls, but genuine feelings and honest vulnerability were clearly off limits, and I had forgotten that our friendship didn't include this kind of talk.

"You'll never get the family to talk to you," Rick says.

"Nobody's going to talk to you," Dave says. "Let's do it."

61

Soon we head to the drive-in, which has been closed for nearly twenty years but lives fresh in our memories as our teenage mecca. Dave finds a torn spot in the rear of a chain-link fence. We squeeze our forty-something bodies through the fence and into the drive-in, which is no longer there. Or to be more accurate, it's here as much as it's not. The screen has been dismantled and hauled away or sold. We're all amazed that since we abandoned the drive-in some twenty-five years ago, trees fifteen and twenty feet high have pushed up through the blacktop, which has become part of a wooded field, wild with weeds. Shoots of trees grow alongside the old speaker poles.

A dog, a boxer, seems disturbed at our arrival. It soon becomes clear that we've encroached on his territory. He circles wide around us, probably as frightened of us as we are of him.

"I hope that dog's friendly," Dave says.

"I wonder if he's been here all winter," Rick says. "He doesn't look hungry or anything, but it looks like he's been living here."

A couple of hundred feet away from where the screen stood there was a snack bar, and off that an efficiency-apartment-sized projectionist's room, home to Floyd, the projectionist and caretaker, and Heidi. Floyd, one sad man; Heidi, one fat dog.

Not much is left of the building. Whole walls are missing. One end of a roof reaches all the way to the floor. Indiscernible graffiti cover the walls that have been left standing. Apparently we're visiting somebody else's past as well as our own.

A pink stuffed elephant, a football, and a plastic chair litter the ground; all carry chew marks. Seeing the dog's toys reminds us to look for him.

"I don't see him anywhere," I say. "Maybe he took off."

"You sure that's not your girlfriend, Joe?" Dave asks.

"No, but I'd do her," I say, enjoying the idiocy of boyhood all over again.

"There he is," Rick says, pointing to the boxer crouching in the snow.

"It's freezing out here, man," I say, hoping to speed up our visit.

Our dialogue amuses me. We're adolescent boys again, exploring ruins. I wouldn't be surprised if one of us suggested bringing food and water back for the dog or taking it home and asking our parents if we can keep it. I realize we're all looking for different things. I'm there to feel the place again, in my ostensible search for answers about . . . About Tom?

I'm beginning to wonder more and more how much this visit is really about Tom at all. He seems more and more to be a warning to me about a life wasted.

Our concern for the lost dog recalls for me the day Rick and I discovered a bird's nest on the ground in a field we roamed as often as the hallways in our homes. No doubt Rick's dogs, Dusty and Spunky, accompanied us on this day's expedition, as they did on so many others. All that survives of that moment are a couple of images. Rick and I discussed what to do.

"How did the nest land with the eggs still whole?"

"Maybe the mother will come back."

"Don't touch the nest or the mother will smell humans and abandon her chicks."

"I think that's an old wives' tale."

"Maybe we should call somebody."

I love us at moments like this. These are gentle boys. These ignorant little boys want life to go on! They want to protect the chicks soon to be born. They probably imagine themselves acting like mothers, standing guard until the shells crack and tiny wet, glossy-ugly heads poke out.

Then we see the older guys J and T. I'm sure we're grateful we have the nest to distract them. These guys need distraction. Usually

63

it amounts to stealing whatever ball we happen to be playing with or grabbing a hat off a head for a little keep-away.

We understand even then that we're separated from these guys by more than a few years. Not everything can be blamed on puberty. These guys have an unnatural attraction to violence that can't be explained by who their parents are or where they live. Perhaps it's in their DNA, though not one of us has a clue what that is. Our world is simpler and smaller than that. You have us, those like us, and assholes. T and J are assholes, pure and simple, through and through.

And yet, years after the incident that's about to happen in a rutted field behind a Spartan Atlantic department store, I see other sides to these two men. On a white-water rafting trip with a bunch of guys, I see that T was a human being after all. He seemed not much different from the rest of us. He had no recollection of the bird's nest in the rutted field. Perhaps other events eclipsed this one. Some ten years after the nest incident, T was driving a car. There was an accident. His best friend died. I believed I saw a softer side of him that day on the white water.

At a graduation party a few years ago that brought together disparate groups of people, J brought along some old photos. Some were of my brother and me, smiling and stupid, sitting next to J's younger brother. One of the photos showed several neighborhood mothers sitting on the bleachers watching one of our Little League baseball games. Three of the women in the photo, including my mother, would be dead in their forties. Still, J's bringing the picture was a nice gesture, perhaps revealing a nostalgic side of him I didn't know existed.

But no softer sides or warm feelings existed that day in the rutted field behind the Spartan Atlantic when J and T came upon two younger boys and two dogs marveling at an abandoned bird's nest with three or four eggs about to be chicks.

"What are you girls looking at?" one of them asked.

We started explaining, partly out of our own excitement and partly, I'm sure, in hopes of distracting them.

Without saying another word, J shoved us out of the way and squashed the eggs with his boot, grinding the orphaned chicks into the ground as if he were putting out an especially resilient cigarette butt.

They laughed and walked away.

Rick and I were frozen in shock. Once they were out of earshot or rock shot, Rick and I screamed at them and threw rocks at their receding backs. They were already on to some other trouble. A little pinball followed by a little shoplifting at our backyard department store was our best guess.

The memory ends here.

As we struggle through the mounds of drive-in snow, I speak details, dialogue, impressions, and reflections into my tape recorder, stuff my memory can't promise to preserve. I understand that it's a rather pathetic attempt to hold on to something that's already gone.

Rick and Dave seem upset at how the place looks, and I'm suddenly sorry I suggested we come here. These old friends didn't need to be dragged out of their comfortable middle age to meander around a dilapidated drive-in in search of memories that are nowhere to be found. Their memories have been tainted by our visit.

The snow covers everything. They seem a little happier when we begin to unearth speakers. There, something of our past still exists.

It's funny that we've been trying to salvage pieces of the drive-in. On a drunken Friday night in our teens, we invaded the place after the show was over and the moviegoers had left. We ripped speakers from poles and smashed them against the concession stand, tore poles out of the ground. In the paper a few days later, we were

65

called "unidentified vandals." We learned we'd destroyed over seventy sites, which would be 140 fewer carloads of customers paying to watch a flick.

"Look at Joe talking to himself," Dave says to Rick, hoping I'll hear him. "It's sad what's happened to him."

Dave has one of the most infectious laughs I've ever heard. It draws people to him. Although Dave grew up on my street, I never really knew him until the two ends of the street united sometime in our midteens, about the same time I started hanging around with Tom. Before then the kids living on Fairlawn Drive between Queens Highway and Hauserman hung out together, and those from the other side of Queens until Fairlawn dead-ended into the Chevy plant played on their end of the street. I guess we were widening our turf at the time. This union of the opposite ends of the street was symbolized by the union of Rick and Kelly. Rick, who's now lifting every plank and brick in search of frozen drive-in speakers, met his wife of twenty years on the far end of the street. Kelly and her brothers grew up right next door to the Ragman. Rick lived on Hauserman, which we all considered the tip of Fairlawn Drive, right across from the armory and the Metroparks. At the time, we all thought it a bit odd that Rick at sixteen was dating a thirteen-year-old girl. He must have known a good thing even then. He's one of the few guys I grew up with who's had any luck with marriage.

Frigid wind bangs hanging sheets of metal against the brick. I look around for the dog. I think I've seen him twice, but both times I'm mistaken. Soon Rick sees him 180 degrees away from where he was at the last sighting.

The temperature has hit sixteen degrees, not counting the wind chill, as we dig through the rubble. We lift the ends of metal sheets that were once part of the roof of the concession stand. Rick, Dave, and I all find the graffiti off-putting, clear evidence that strangers have painted their present on our past. Or perhaps the graffiti symbolize somebody else's past being superimposed on ours. We discover other things. Paw prints. Ripped-up mattresses. Unidentifiable animal feces.

As they dig in the ruins of our teens, Dave and Rick recall for me a day early in our drinking and early in our driving. The three of us and another friend, Mick, were in my Volkswagen, too drunk to be in a car and flying through the iced-over parking lot of the Spartan Atlantic department store. Because the lot was huge and rarely full, there was a lot of room for drunken doughnuts. Because the engine of a 1966 Volkswagen was in the back, I was able to do some fine spinning. Unfortunately the car could do little else – braking on ice, for example. As we sped down the parking lot toward the always traffic-jammed Brookpark Road, the border of Cleveland, I couldn't stop. There were cars everywhere. Soon the Bug was filled with screams of "oh, fuck" and "holy shit" and "we're dead."

And then it happened.

"It was like the Red Sea parting," Rick recalls. "It was like God's hand coming down and parting the cars for us."

With the waters of steel moved out of the way, we slipped directly across Brookpark Road and safely to the other side. When we turned around to see what we'd passed through, the lanes had refilled with cars.

"Do you believe that?" I ask Rick. "That God intervened and saved us that night?"

"Absolutely. What else was it?" Rick asks. "There were cars everywhere. I closed my eyes for a second, and then we were on the other side of the street. I turned around, cars everywhere."

I don't want to admit to Rick and Dave that I don't believe the hand of God reached down and parted the Brookpark Road traffic for our inebriated passage, so I don't say anything.

Dave wants to visit his dad, who's battling cancer and still living in the house on Fairlawn, so he says good-bye and Rick and I grab some lunch. Dave, who keeps Harleys parked in his front room and is covered with tattoos of a grizzly bear ripping through his skin, a saber-tooth, a scorpion, a Chinese dragon, a fireball, and a deer he added just beyond the grizzly's reach, is convinced that prayers have saved his father, who is suddenly gaining weight and feeling better long after doctors thought he wouldn't be around. May I remind you – as I have to remind myself – that Dave is not an "all we need is prayer," "it's God's will" kind of Christian. I'm not even sure he'd call himself a Christian at all. I do know that he believes in God and in the power of prayer.

On this strange day, I know I do not. I do know that I want to feel the faith they have. What these old friends possess is not exactly the "faith of our fathers," but it's faith nonetheless. To put these guys in the same camp as TV evangelists would be to completely misunderstand their generation-worn, blue-collar-cut religion.

Despite the ostensible gains I've achieved since fleeing this neighborhood all those years ago, I know nothing has made me as content as I desire to be. I'm only beginning to realize how much I've lost.

After lunch Rick asks if I want to see the place where Tom died. Of course I do. I follow Rick onto the highway and to West 130. All the while I'm trying to figure out why we're not better friends. We've always gotten along. We seem to talk as easily now as when we were twelve. Hell, we were best friends as kids. We're both nostalgic and romantic about our childhoods. We share a past, a love of family, and . . . I'm sure there are other things. I want to say just shut up, Mr. forty-four-year-old trapped in a pubescent mind. Please grow the fuck up. So you're not great friends anymore. Who is? Who needs friends in middle age the way you needed them during puberty? Right?

Rick pulls off the freeway at 130th, and I follow him. I try to focus on everything I see. This stretch of 130th has earned a reputation as one of the worst drug corners on Cleveland's west side. It's no real surprise that Tom spent his last days here. The area reminds me of visiting junkyards with my dad. My dad saw a way to save money. All I saw were broken-down cars, battered front ends and smashed windows – of cars that were the sole witnesses to a teenager's last Friday night out – and the oil-stained fingers of fat men who ignored kids visiting junkyards with their dads and apparently worshipped naked women wielding wrenches on out-of-date calendars.

It seems momentous that in only a few seconds I'll be face-to-face with the spot where Tom died. I half expect to see a white cross. We pull to the side of the street and get out of our cars.

"I think he was parked in back," Rick says. "Right over there."

It's about one o'clock on a Saturday afternoon, and the place is closed. Because of the cold, not too many people are out and about unless they're in their cars. But there's one guy, about our age, maybe a little younger, walking around, looking at us. He's hammered, tripping off the curb, bumping into it as if it's a four-foot wall. His hair hangs in streaky tails from under his knit hat. His goatee looks to be home to several species of fauna once thought extinct. He asks us if we need anything. God knows why. Perhaps we've ventured into his territory. My first thought is that maybe this guy knew Tom. Hell, they could have been drinking buddies.

I think again of Tom. No doubt he shared a few of this guy's desires and demons. Even Tom's looks couldn't have been much better in the final days. He seems to be a vestige of Tom, some kind of corporeal reminder and a spectral presence at the same time. This is a guy like Tom. A guy like me. He too has a story. If I asked this guy what he was before he was a drunk, he might just answer, a kid.

Two days after my visit here with Rick, I call the lot that was closed on Saturday. I dial the phone asking not about used cars, bad credit, or generous financing but about a dead friend. I'm told that the owner, Deano – yeah, Deano – is in Vegas and won't be back for a few days yet.

"Well maybe you can help me," I say to the salesman on the phone. "A friend of mine worked at R&C, and I was told he died there."

"What was his name?"

"Tom McGinty."

"McGinty?" he asks. I wonder if he's suddenly fearing a lawsuit or an enraged relative. "You say he worked here? Who are you again?"

I tell him I'm an old friend of Tom's.

"How long ago was this?"

"Summer of 1997, I think. How long have you worked there?"

"I've been here for around eight years. Don't know anybody named McGinty."

"What about a Tom?"

"No."

"A lot of people called him the Ragman."

"The Ragman. No. The only guy I know who was found dead around here was some guy they found in his kitchen. He'd been dead for days. Cats were eating him."

Goddamnit, please, I think, don't let the guy be talking about Tom.

I thank him for his time and tell him I'll call again when Deano's back from Vegas.

I'm discovering that nobody can give me any solid details of

Tom's death or of his final days. Even his closest friends have him dying of several different diseases.

Rick and I stand around in the cold for a few minutes, bouncing from foot to foot trying to get warm.

We shake hands good-bye and drive off.

As I honk and pull into traffic, I look in my rearview mirror and see my reflection superimposed, for just a second, on the tail-haired drunk, stumbling down the street.

6

Not long after I visit the drive-in with Rick and Dave, I decide it's time to take a closer look at the home of my youth. So little has changed. Because it's brick, I don't have to face a house of a different color. The tree that once rose like a leafy haven in the front yard has been cut down, as has the small plum tree my dad planted. Tiny red awnings overhang the windows. The fence still stands. Different cars sit in the driveway. Different residents live their own lives, not wanting to be bothered by a forty-something guy looking for something he can't even define.

Regardless of who wants me to or whose privacy I'm invading, I pull past the driveway that was once mine and park in front of the house. The driveway served as the site of two of my most memorable early experiences with the power of language:

I stand at the edge of my suburban driveway on Fairlawn Drive, sunny and safe. Mick and I are playing Whiffle ball. Each swing of the bat sends the ball flying into the mystery grip of physics and aerodynamic wonder. The ball appears to be headed straight up before some hidden hand of wind and speed and serrated plastic jerks it deeper out and over to the lawn of the widow next door. Mrs. Worth's boxer drools the day away, watching from the backyard in its own state of ignorant awe. We take turns smacking the shit out of the plastic ball. I don't notice right away that an older kid – a man really – is walking down the other side of the street, his eyes straight ahead. Not from around here. As the kid-man gets closer, I focus more intently on the game, as if this focus will protect me from what's about to happen. I chase the ball as if catching it matters more than anything, more than my first kiss or my last day of school. I make careful throws, keeping my eye on the ball, trying to anticipate the direction of its flight and fall.

I fear – as I so often fear – that something I've done has found its way back to me and now I'll pay. Five or six houses away now, the kid-man crosses the street. He's not from around here, but I recognize him from somewhere. There's something in the way he never looks around, as if his entire world centers on a horizon only he can see. He's smoking. Not a good sign. I pick the ball up off the boxer's drool-wet lawn, wipe it on my jeans, and toss it a few feet in the air. When I look up I see the kid-man – black hair greased and straight, a broken mustache, patches of dirt and beard – punch Mick square in the nose. In one motion Mick bends over and covers his nose with cupped hands. Blood oozes through his summer-stained fingers and drips onto the hot concrete. Although the kid-man – eighteen, nineteen, probably – has just punched Mick in the face, I'm stunned stupid when he walks over and slams me in the face too. We run to the porch.

"My girlfriend's not a dyke," he says, as he lights a new cigarette from the old and walks away.

Now I realize where I've seen him. He's going out with a girl at the end of the street. And it's true: we have called his girlfriend a dyke. Often and repeatedly. But still, standing behind the harsh, cool-sounding word with blood dripping from my nose, I – who only five minutes ago was playing Whiffle ball on a summer afternoon – realize I can't define the word we all so love to use.

On another summer day, also a Whiffle ball day, I call one of my Gentile friends a dumb Jew. This new way of degrading each other catches on quickly. Not one of the Catholic boys schooled in the Judeo-Christian tradition is sure why calling somebody a dumb Jew is derogatory. But we revel in this new slur anyway. But wait. Wasn't Jesus a Jew? Isn't Bill Rosenberg a Jew? We all love Bill. This must be something else. It sounds different. It sounds like it shouldn't be said. So we say it and love saying it, we boys without weapons.

The screen door slams. My mother has caught the sound of the slur. She motions for me to come inside. "Tell your friends to go home," she says.

I don't have to. They're gone. This is 1971, and the suburbs. Somebody's parent is everybody's parent. Parents stick together. They know who the real enemy is.

She grabs my hair and pulls me into the house. Inside my head I'm screaming, "Take it easy. Get your hands off me!"

I don't say a word.

"What did you say out there? What were you saying?"

I understand that my mother knows the answers to her questions. I realize I had better not repeat what I said outside, not even to answer her. I know she never wants to hear that again. Not ever. Not from me. Not from anybody.

"Where did you ever hear a thing like that? That kind of talk?" she asks.

An excellent question. I honestly don't know. I think for a moment more. I have no idea.

The slur just seems to have been out there, there and somehow not there, like incense, like the way a Whiffle ball whips and dips, the way adults laugh at things kids don't understand, the way background noise from baseball games leaks out of transistor radios, the way bits of gravel bounce out of pickup truck beds, the way factory fires flirt with the night sky, the way sonic booms burst the lie of silence.

The people who live here now must have just returned home, because they all happen to be getting out of their car. They regard me through eyes that seem suspicious. A teenage boy and his father – I assume it's his father – head into the house, no longer showing any interest in my presence in their driveway. The woman, however, walks over to me as I attempt to explain why I'm there.

The family is Indian or Pakistani. I'm ashamed to admit I can't be certain of the difference. I introduce myself and tell her I grew up in their house and would like to take a few pictures if she doesn't mind. She immediately turns wary.

"Why do you need to take pictures?" she asks. "It's not your house anymore. It's different." A large diamond pierces the side of her nose and is accented by her black hair.

"The house looks great," I tell her, although I really do not notice too many changes, nor am I looking for any. I'm looking for what has not changed. The house is still a brick ranch with an unattached garage. My dad built the garage after we'd lived without one for several years. Plus, nearly every house on the street has the same design, built by the same builder. Floor plan: front room, dining room, kitchen, down the hallway to three bedrooms and a bath. And of course a basement, which everyone living in this place in the seventies rushed to "finish."

"When we bought the house there was dog shit in the backyard," she says.

I tell her I'll only be here for a minute or two. She nods, but her arms are crossed and she watches me, then follows me. She has every right, of course, to not trust me. She's smart to be at least a little suspicious of my presence. After all, this is Parma, strong on patriotism and xenophobia, and a bad place to have dark skin. I have no idea what her life has been like since September 11 or if she has suffered any injustices. Why would she? She's not some terrorist from Saudi Arabia. She didn't fly planes into buildings or crash them in fields. But to some eyes she undoubtedly looks like the people who did. And that's usually enough.

Whatever the case, she clearly wants me gone. I quickly snap shot after shot, careful not to point the camera directly at the house. Instead I focus on the view toward the empty field and the back of a blue-light department store. I also take shots of the garage, of the heat pipe poking up through the back.

(After our family moved out of the house and my dad was renting it to another couple, I broke in every night for a week or so, raiding the refrigerator for leftover pizza and cold beer. The couple had not officially taken up residence, and I needed a place to sleep. Plus, I figured I had squatter's rights.)

I thank the Indian or Pakistani woman for letting me wander through her backyard. Again she asks me what I'm doing and why I need to take pictures. She asks if I'm from the insurance company or the bank.

The metal gate squeaks as I leave, and I want to hear it squeak again.

"Thank you. Have a good day," I say, trying to sound as innocuous as possible.

I watch her watch me drive off.

All the time I'm there, I'm trying to feel something. I wish the woman would trust me enough to let me roam around. But even freedom to roam would most likely not have helped. In all honesty, I don't feel a thing. I was hoping for a semblance of authentic emotion. I've been coming around this street enough lately to admit to myself that perhaps my ability to relive this place on an emotional level is just flat out of my reach.

As I turn my eyes back to the road, I catch sight of the old Benny place, two doors down from where I grew up. The kids' names were Marco, Kathy, and Mike. They were a nice family. When I was about twelve, they took a vacation to Canada. The family came back without Mr. Benny, who had drowned somewhere. For years I associated Canada with drowning. It became the country where families go to drown. The Bennys moved away shortly after the drowning.

When my own family visited the country on the other side of Lake Erie for several years running, I often thought of Mr. Benny. I saw him driving up to Canada, going out on a boat, falling into the water. I watched him never come home. I often wondered what would happen to our family if my father drowned in Canada.

When I was a kid, my family rented a cottage on Ontario's Trent River for sixty dollars a week. My father, my brother, and I would wake up every morning at five o'clock. My mother and two sisters stayed in the cottage, playing games, making breakfast, killing bugs. Our goal was to catch the beautiful and powerful northern pike, but we happily settled for jumbo perch or large- and small-mouth bass. There was nothing like the rush of seeing a baseball-sized bobber disappearing in an instant and then fighting the fish up to the surface and into the boat. I caught a two-foot-long northern pike one summer and had it mounted. My ten-year-old brother – the funniest person I know and now a comedian, voice-over artist, and writer in Los Angeles – made jokes about "mounting" the fish right there in the boat. My dad usually ignored the sexual innuendo coming from his youngest son. Sometimes he would turn to me and ask why he said things like that. I'd shake my head while laughing like a lunatic on crack.

One day my whole family – minus my mother – went out on our small rowboat. There were too many of us. The Trent River sported small whitecaps from motorboats passing too close and too fast. We four kids were jostling too much in the boat. Oars banged the sides. I heard a splash, then I saw the lime-green sweatshirt of my three-year-old sister sinking in the river. I leaned over the side and watched her descend. My dad dived into the river, straight down, grabbed my baby sister, and held her above his head as first she then he broke the surface. She screamed, gasped, sobbed, choked, and spat. And then another sound broke the afternoon air. My father's laughter. A wild, chaotic, brilliant, unending laugh. My dad shook with laughter as he cared for and comforted my sister. With Mary screaming and gasping and sobbing and choking and spitting and my dad laughing, he could hardly row the boat. The river carried his laugh on its lighted surface. The laughter shimmered in the sun, luminescent, so that passersby turned and pointed. My dad's laughter seemed to hang on every tree branch and cover every rock and root. It was as vast and as timeless as the river, as wet and wild as the whitecaps. Soon everybody in the boat began laughing. Even my almost-drowned sister laughed. I laughed too, but I didn't completely understand my dad's laughing. Of course he was excited and grateful, and no doubt he had a mean adrenaline rush. My sister was fine now. We all had survived a close call. We are the Mackall family, not the Benny family. But still I found my father's laughter odd and a bit disturbing. After all, he laughed even while his frightened almost-drowned, just-saved daughter cried. He laughed through the gray confusion and crazy grace of the moment. I decided to give myself completely to my family's laughter and all it did and did not mean.

On one vacation to the Trent River, my mother caught a six-pound, eighteen-inch largemouth bass. It's now pinned to a wall in my dad's house, its tail frozen in midleap, its mouth open wide, still lunging for life twenty-five years after the fisherwoman's death.

A half mile away I arrive at St. Bridget's Church and School; I know it's a half mile because I walked or biked it every school day for nine years. I check the side doors of the church first. The first side door is locked; so is the other one. A church should never be locked, I say aloud to nobody. The main doors, the doors I check last, are unlocked. Why do I always try to enter Catholic churches from the side? Why do I feel the need to slither in?

In my darkest days as a practicing atheist, I often visited this church between services, sitting alone, listening to the wooden pews groaning and creaking under the weight of years. I'd sit near the front of the church and curse it for all its failings and hypocrisy and blind dogma and then, if I wasn't careful, would long for the faith I had as a child.

But that was long ago.

On this day I bring a tiny glass bottle from the inside of a crucifix. My wife bought it for me a Christmas or two ago because it was identical to one we had in the hallway of my boyhood home. I want holy water from Saint Bridget's church. A memento from when blessed water meant something to me, when I loved to feel its cool, sacred presence on my forehead. A keepsake. Nothing but nostalgia manifest. I unscrew the cap and dip the thumb-size bottle into the font. When I pull it out, it's empty. I dip again. Empty. I look around the church as if I'm the brunt of some cosmic joke. This time I cover the mouth of the bottle with my finger, lower it into the water, remove my finger, and let it fill. I cap the bottle and leave.

I make my way to the school. It's after hours. Not a student around. I walk into the boys' restroom. Time has not touched the urinals, the stalls, the sinks, or the tile floor.

If I hadn't lain stomach down on this very bathroom floor with my friend Jeff on a spring afternoon thirty years ago, I doubt I would be a college professor today. I was going to flunk math. Jeff and I were going to flunk math. In order not to flunk, we had to solve some fifty pages of math problems and complete them with a passing grade. We had one day to do it. I knew this was impossible.

I had a one-way ticket to flunking-math-ville. I was done. I'd have to repeat eighth grade.

I'd be stuck behind with a bunch of seventh graders and a cotillion of nuns who knew I'd flunked out. I'd have to hear lectures from Sister Gerald about how my flunking math was all part of God's plan. I'd have to listen to Sister Concepta – unaffectionately referred to as "Cun the nun" – ridicule my attempt at academic subterfuge and announce loudly and publicly that in all her years of teaching grade school nothing good had ever come out of the boys' bathroom.

But Jeff had a plan, and I went along with it willingly. Somehow – perhaps from his older brother, Larry, who would soon cause an explosion in his bedroom when a science experiment went awry – Jeff had acquired the answers to all the problems we were given to solve. So after school one day, when we should have been at band practice, or church, or home, or a baseball scrimmage, we stretched out on the bathroom floor and filled in the answers to our problems, being careful not to get them all right and taking turns writing down wrong answers. I have no idea how we got away with this. I do not remember a single person's entering the bathroom. There was no fallout from our math teacher, whom I recall as a smart and decent young man. We didn't graduate with any distinction or honor, but we did walk with our class. I'd been schooled in Catholicism long enough by then to know that we had cheated like hell, and in hell we were sure to burn.

But hell's a long way off when you're thirteen.

As a grade-school student with a mad stutter, I took in thousands and thousands of words, but very few actually made it out of my mouth, and almost none burst into the atmosphere unscathed. When they did make it out they landed in pieces, lying in the listener's ear like shattered bits of language lost, parts of speech.

My parents assumed my stutter was psychological, in keeping with the science of the day. After all, I stuttered much less in small groups of family or close friends. But school was where language went to die. I hated the drill of students' reading successive paragraphs. I was always counting ahead, students and paragraphs, praying – it was a Catholic school after all – that my assigned paragraph would be mercifully pithy. Subject, verb, object, nothing more. Invariably, it seemed, I'd get the longest damn paragraph in the book. Reading while standing up in front of the class was the worst, because then I could not hide the punches I inflicted on my thighs in hopes of jarring words loose. My free arm acted like a Parkinson's-stricken metronome, keeping time in a controlled self-abuse – pinching, punching, slamming my legs, the top of the desk, anything to set the words free. Nothing seemed to help.

(I was a boy who lived in a constant imaginative fog. I read for hours every day. I took in bits and pieces of reality only to lose them, and everything I lost got subsumed into an imagination that was all-consuming, yet not first-rate. I made life into story in a desperate attempt to understand something I could not seem to understand any other way. Maybe going back "home" is a way of reclaiming my life from story. Or maybe, once again, it's all about story. Maybe I just don't like the way death seemed to end my story of growing up prematurely. Maybe I don't think it's over at all. Or as Mikal Gilmore writes, "It is death that tells us that a story's ended – that it is now time to evaluate the life that is finished, to reckon its plot and its drama, and to tell its stories.")

My grade-school years were defined by my love-hate relationship with reading and words. I loved reading silently more than any other activity on earth, and I loved to write while the stutter slumbered. When I was ten years old, I wrote my own version of the Hardy Boys stories, only with girl detectives. The nuns promised me I could read a chapter to the class. I talked one of my friends into agreeing to read my words to my mates. What a vindication this would be! But before that could happen, I had to read aloud from a text. The passage was excruciatingly long. Perhaps because of the extra excitement of anticipating hearing my own words read smoothly and effortlessly by a classmate, I suffered one of the worst stuttering experiences of my life. It took me so long to read the text that my fifth-grade teacher informed me I had taken up too much of our day. We had no time to read my chapter. God, how I loathed reading aloud. I almost felt for my teachers and my fellow students. How long I kept them all waiting! My botched and broken reading aloud tested the patience and Christian forbearance of my teacher nuns, most of whom told me just to stop stuttering and read. Convincing them I read several books a week was impossible. My language skill betrayed me – denied it knew me the way Peter betrayed Christ before the cock crowed its acoustically telling trinity. Is this why nuns looked at me the way they did? One in particular, Sister Concepta, my sixth-grade science teacher, finally broke. She hated me for my poor conduct and my inconvenient stutter. She broke six times in all. The rumor was that she had had six nervous breakdowns. I assumed I surely must have been responsible for at least one or two. Take that, bitch!

As I walk out of the school building, my fingertips rub against the wall. The brickwork looks the same. I wonder if brick holds memory the way brain tissue does.

Although I grew up telling myself I would never establish roots, that I would sever the ties that held me in childhood, that to stay put was to perish, I now believe differently. Now, returning to the places of my "blood ties," I cannot help but feel loss in the marrow of my memory, as if I had once been banished from my homeland and long to return. And of course in a way I have been banished. Time is the great leveler of exile. Time says who comes, who goes, and who stays. I cannot get back, even by going back. You need time and place together for there to be a blood tie. Revisit a tree in whose bark you and a young lover carved a promise of love. The initials might be there, but the love and at least one lover are not.

What would I give for one more fall afternoon of innocence! My God, kissing the cool cheek of a childhood girlfriend, watching her lithe legs mottle red in the cold, loving the way she wears a sweater and shorts in the cool of autumn, dreaming a hundred dreams in a day. Maybe I'll marry her and we could. . . . Or she will miss me when I choose another and will remember me on late fall afternoons when she looks out her bay window as cars pass on an excruciatingly ordinary Wednesday. In the morning I would dream of becoming a policeman, by afternoon a psychiatrist; early evening would find me fantasizing the life of an anthropologist, and in the middle of the night, the time and place of true dreams and fears, I'd think about being a writer so that I could hold all these dreams and all these people, and all these girls with cool cheeks and mottled legs. And do it quickly before we all vanish, in cars that are not ours, on late August afternoons when not a single soul is watching.

I walk in the cold from the school to the rectory. The nun in the school office told me that Mrs. Mary Maloney, a great family friend and as much a part of the parish as goosebumps on the uniformed legs of grade-school girls, was helping out at the rectory. For at least a generation she had worked in the school office, treating every student as if he or she were truly a son or daughter of God, which is not something I can say of all of the clergy who walked the same halls.

I ring the doorbell of the rectory. I feel I want a thousand answers to a thousand questions, but I don't know where to begin. A priest I don't recognize answers the door. I can't help thinking that priests probably don't open doors with the aplomb they once did. Perhaps this man fears I'm one more altar boy turned apostate who had been abused on a retreat and has returned seeking retribution.

"Hello, Father," I say. "I was wondering if I could talk to Mrs. Maloney."

As I walk into the too-warm rectory, Mrs. Maloney gives me the look of not knowing, and then comes recognition. She gives me a hug and introduces me to the priest, whose name I have forgotten.

"This is Joe Mackall," Mrs. Maloney tells the priest. "The Mackall kids all went to school here. They spent their summers in our pool. Mrs. Mackall died so young."

My childhood story in a few sentences, ending with my mother's early death.

Mrs. Maloney looks at me with an expression that suggests she wants me to speak my mother's age so she doesn't get it wrong.

"She was forty-four," I say. "My age now." As I say this I realize I'm actually forty-five now. Something seems to be stuck.

Mrs. Maloney starts telling me about her grandchildren and her stroke. I can still make out her pretty Irish face beneath her aged skin and stroke-deformed muscles. We all still call her Mrs. Maloney, even though she technically has not been a wife for over a quarter of a century. Mr. Maloney also died in his early forties. He gave most of his young years to a company that made millions manufacturing asbestos. Asbestosis killed a good young man who left behind a wife and young children. The company denied any wrongdoing and turned its back on its workers. Nobody got a dime. One more blue-collar story that begins with love and loyalty and ends with death and apathy.

"So what brings you back here?" Mrs. Maloney asks.

"I'm just curious about the old neighborhood," I say, unsure. "I've been thinking about my mom, and Tom McGinty dying and . . ."

"I heard about that. That was awful." Mrs. Maloney's sadness seems to have sunk into the side of her face that's distorted by her stroke.

"I think something went wrong in our neighborhood," I say.

Although I don't know why, I look at the priest when I say this.

I suppose I'm hoping he'll be interested in what I'm doing. Perhaps he can be of some help. After all, so many of my generation have struggled with or given up on the faith of our fathers. Even the middle-aged believers are at best cafeteria Catholics, picking and choosing from the buffet of beliefs. "I'll take life everlasting, but I'm not touching that birth control ban." And with the Catholic Church being on the ropes lately, I guess I thought a young priest might be curious about what I was trying to do.

"It was nice meeting you," Father says to me. "I'd better get back to work."

Mrs. Maloney and I trade questions about the health and welfare of our respective family members for a time. After that's over, I realize I'm having trouble explaining to her and to myself what I'm doing standing in the foyer of the rectory, making small talk with a woman I haven't seen in years.

Our little reunion ends with a hug from Mrs. Maloney and a promise that I'll stay in touch.

I walk out of the rectory and gaze into the grove across the parking lot. I used to love perching on a picnic table amid the pine trees. Picnic tables and pine trees still grace the grove. Sometimes while sitting there I'd perform a bit of mental magic. I'd close my eyes and imagine everything around me disappearing down a huge hole. First the grove, school, church, and neighborhood were gone. Cities, highways, oceans, and countries followed. Then planets, moon, the sun and stars. Soon all of history never happened. I imagined a vast nothingness. But not nothingness, exactly. Only God remained, or at least what I was calling God those days in the grove. There never had to be anything, I'd tell myself. Nothing ever had to exist. Even when I convinced myself that nothing existed, there was still something there. This is what I told myself. But it wasn't only in my imagination that I experienced this. I could feel the thing that was there when nothing else existed; my head would fill with something resembling an elastic dizziness. I've never been able to feel this as an adult. I could always imagine a disappearing world, but I could never again feel the divine existence that remained behind. Maybe, I told myself, this was nothing more than the result of growing up.

Bare tree branches reach over the corners of the school building, as if they're propping up the roof-topping cumulus clouds. A stone cross sits between the trees. One part of me wants to sprint around the snow-covered bases on Blair Field, run through the hallways of St. Bees looking for lost friends, rush to the library to retrieve our Dalmatian the day he'd chased a nun onto a tabletop, help one ancient nun move the desks out of the way so she could box the biggest clown in class, hold hands with girls and boys as we circled the statue of the Virgin Mary on a May afternoon filled with the joy of a school year's final days.

But I don't linger.

I walk back to my car on one more frigid day, wishing for some kind of authentic emotional reaction to my brief visit with Mrs. Maloney. I had such high hopes.

But I do feel something.

I pull my coat closed at the neck and swear my chest aches from asbestosis.

7

I don't even try to see Tom's family until the summer after meeting with Rick and Dave in the drive-in that bitter January day. Maybe it's partly because of their warnings about the family's unwillingness to talk about Tom. But the past year or so I've noticed how long it takes me to do anything. How little I really want to do. At times I'm sorry I started going back to the old neighborhood. Its weight has bogged me down. Nothing's working out the way I dreamed it would. I'm not any closer to understanding how I changed in the years leading up to and after my mother's death. I'm no closer to understanding who she was or why it matters that I look back to her now. I don't know what meaning I'm supposed to find in Tom's death. I'm no nearer to comprehending the loss that seems to have dogged my life. Friendships have resisted rekindling. I do not feel what I had hoped to feel – reconnection.

And I'm closer to having a drink than I've been in over sixteen years.

I call Tom's sister anyway.

Tom's youngest sister, Ruthanne, ostensibly is pleased to hear from me. She tells me she'd be happy to talk about Tom.

I arrive at Ruthanne's Parma home on a Friday afternoon deep in summer. I thought she and I would be talking alone, but I soon see there are McGintys everywhere. Her parents are up from Florida. Her sister is in from another Cleveland suburb. Her two sons soon arrive. One brings along his girlfriend and their baby. Ruthanne seems delighted to be a forty-two-year-old grandmother.

For a time we're all out on the screened-in porch getting reacquainted. The clamor of kids and grandkids forces us inside, for which I'm grateful.

Ruthanne proudly shows me the pictures of her six kids adorning a wall in the front room. I admire her ability to showcase six kids from three marriages with the same pride some Stepford wife might take in her two-point-three kids from the one man in her life. The way her grown sons treat her, it's obvious she's a good and loving mother.

As we begin to talk, I'm struck to hear Ruthanne and her older sister, Maryann, say that Tom is far better off dead than he ever was alive. Although it's clear to me that they loved their brother and miss him, his life was simply too hard for him and his family to take for any longer.

"He was always drunk," Maryann says as she holds a beer can in one hand and a cigarette in the other. "He'd get up in the morning and drink Wild Irish Rose all day long."

"When he was in intensive care for two weeks a couple of months before he died, the doctor told him that if he didn't quit drinking he was going to kill himself," Ruthanne says. "Tommy said, 'I know.'"

The two sisters go back and forth like this for a while. I learn that Tommy's nickname came from his penchant for garbage picking when he was a kid. His dad dubbed Tom the Ragman, and the moniker stuck.

"When Tommy was living in Lakewood, he kept saying he heard voices in the walls and ceiling," Maryann says. "He used to bang a broom into the ceiling."

"It went downhill when Mom and Dad moved to Florida. Tommy was a momma's boy. He lost the security when they moved."

Ruthanne tells how her father began making homemade wine when Tom was thirteen or fourteen. Tom took an immediate liking to the basement-aged nectar.

"He just couldn't get out of that fucking wine," she says.

On an end table in the living room is a picture of the McGinty kids: Marty, the oldest boy, Maryann, and Ruthanne. The picture clearly was taken after Tom's death, so Ruthanne has tucked an old picture of Tom in the corner of the frame.

Marty McGinty works as a firefighter for the Cleveland Fire Department. When I spoke to him weeks earlier, he remembered who I was and displayed no overt surprise at my calling.

"I'm real sorry about Tom, Marty," I said.

"That's okay."

"I always really liked Tom. He was a good guy," I said, struggling to say more.

"Yeah, he was," Marty said. "He just couldn't outrun his demons."

Marty informed me that he was extremely busy and couldn't see me for a couple of months. Until then he'd be working full time at the firehouse and part time at Jacob's Field and had a lot to do with the department's honor guard.

I can't help thinking that Marty wanted me to know how busy he was, how full his life is, which was of course not at all true for Tom.

"Marty told me Tom just couldn't outrun his demons," I say.

"Once I had to shoot my gun through the roof just to scare Tommy, he was so drunk," Maryann says, lighting another cigarette.

After more tales of Tom's drunken exploits like driving his car through the back of a garage, Ruthanne recalls that Tom had no clothes to be buried in. His folks had to buy a suit, new socks, shoes, clean underwear.

Soon the talk changes a bit. The sisters' love for their lost brother is obvious, but there's something else unfolding as well.

Maryann says she had a "funny feeling" the day Tom died, long before she knew the day would be her brother's last.

Ruthanne had a prenatal doctor's appointment that day. She'd been pregnant for nearly three months, and today would be the day she and her third husband, Allen, first heard the baby's heartbeat.

"We had the appointment, went home, and my son Tommy said, 'Uncle Tom's dead,'" Ruthanne says.

Talk turns to the mysterious ways of God and how it had all been planned that some shard of Tom's soul would be present in this new baby.

Although I don't remember all that was said that day, I do know I was becoming increasingly uncomfortable with talk of God's ways and shared souls. The women talked of Maryann's "funny feeling" and Ruthanne's baby daughter's heartbeat as signs from God. I had stopped taking notes. As discomfited as I was, I didn't want the women to feel I was judging them by my silence, so I offered an anecdote of my own.

When I had been visiting my mother's grave in my early twenties, just a few years after her death, clouds hung over Holy Cross Cemetery. Cloudy days in Cleveland are, of course, nothing unusual. I believe it's been partly cloudy since about 1950. On this day, as I stood over my mother's grave, refusing to pray, not even for her, not ever again, the sun punctured the clouds for a brief moment, and the gravestone caught the rays, reflecting the sun into my eyes, forcing them shut and in effect blinding me for a second.

"It was bizarre," I say lamely.

"See, that was your mom telling you that everything was okay," Ruthanne says.

I don't admit to any burning bush experience, but I want to meet the women's open vulnerability with a little vulnerability of my own.

The difference was this: they believed in their signs, and I did not.

When I finish telling my tale, I suddenly recall a moment that must have lain quiet in memory for over thirty years.

My family and I were on our way to Canada. I was ten or twelve, my mother in her mid-thirties.

I forget what began the discussion, but soon I gathered the guts to open up to her.

"I don't think I believe in God," I said.

My mother was a militant Catholic with an explosive temper, so I knew I was risking something by this public disavowal of my faith. When I got an F in religion at my Catholic grade school, you'd have thought I'd sodomized the pope. My failing grade was the result of constant screwing around in class and being unable to write cogently about what I'd read in the Catholic rag *The Universe Bulletin*. When I got my F, my mother grounded me for an entire semester. I remember shooting baskets alone in my driveway for hours, days, weeks, months during my incarceration, often hearing my mother screaming out the dining room window, "My son the atheist!"

So when I told her I no longer believed in God, I expected the worst. I prepared for a fight.

But I didn't get one.

"Why don't you believe in God anymore?" she asked. "Did something happen?"

I began telling her about the presence of evil in the world and how could it possibly matter whether I ate meat on Friday and an assortment of other complaints about Catholicism and injustice.

My mother didn't argue with me. She didn't get upset. She listened. Soon I exhausted my lapsarian litany and just said again, "I don't believe in God."

In a calm and loving voice, my mother said, "Maybe someday you will."

I was astonished. Perhaps my mother just outsmarted me that day, or maybe she herself had had serious doubts once upon a time. I'll never know.

Sometimes, when I look back at my childhood, it seems to me I wanted few things more than to not believe, to denounce the faith I'd been reared in.

I didn't say anything else to my mom about my atheism that day, and I don't recall if she said anything more.

All I know is that she listened to me say I didn't believe. If I'd said this to a nun or priest at school, someone would have called my parents in for a serious discussion, no doubt blaming my home life for my sinful ways.

When I think of my mother now, I think of that moment in the car, a moment I hadn't thought about until I began revisiting Fairlawn Drive.

Then Ruthanne shows me something I'd never seen before: a photograph of Tom lying in his coffin. I don't ask why somebody would take a photo like this; I just smile.

Yes, it's Tom. No, it's not.

And then it begins to happen. I look around the room as if I'm floating above us all. I'm not finding out a thing I didn't know about Tom. All his sisters can really give me are their own views of Tom and a few more anecdotes of how bad things were with him. I didn't know Tom heard voices. I didn't know he'd almost died a few months before he did. His parents don't seem to want to talk about him.

I imagine Tom's final moments. I find myself fantasizing about the inebriated oblivion he disappeared into.

How does a thirty-seven-year-old man who was once a boy die in his car clutching an empty cigarette pack? Maybe it was something as common as the cracks in the concrete or the grease in the streets that cursed the Ragman to this lonely death without dreams. Maybe blame rests in the molecular fumes from the Chevy plant that wafted over us and then away like lost faith. Or maybe the Ragman picked the time and place himself.

Speaking euphemistically, overly generously, the Ragman was not comfortable with capitalism. He was chronically unemployed. Even his sisters will tell you as much. Booze became his balm, drugs his unholy grail. In our predominately Irish Catholic neighborhood, if the church, its dogma, and its comforts didn't work for you, alcohol and drugs often stepped in to fill the void, and voids seemed as ubiquitous as the sewer grates that swallowed our wayward baseballs. Tom lived his life as a sacramental boozer, a chemical pilgrim.

And it seems the story of Tom is already being told. Ruthanne will tell her grandchildren that their great-uncle Tom was a guy with a big heart and some talent as a mechanic. And then she'll tell them how drink and drugs destroyed his life, and there will be talk about how shards of Tom's soul live on in a baby whose heartbeat was heard for the first time on the day Tom died. There will be some speculation about what Tom could have been, if only.

Tom's sisters continue talking, but I'm not listening. Instead I'm thinking of a distant uncle I never met. All I heard from relatives were jokes about his legendary drinking. What I didn't know until years later was that he had fought in World War I and World War II. For some reason, the wars were left out of his story.

As I sit in Ruthanne's home, hovering, with a picture of Tom in his casket in front of me, I think back to Rick's words to me: "Tom was a good guy. He was just fucked up." A life in two sentences.

I could locate Tom's ex-wife and ask her to talk about falling in love with Tom and what she saw, but I don't think that will get me anywhere. Hell, I'm not sure I'd want somebody getting the low-down on me from my ex-wife, although we've been good friends for over twenty years now. And talking to Tom's estranged son is out of the question. Leave him be, is what I hear in my head.

"Tom was always good to me," I say to Ruthanne as I hand the photo album to her.

"It stormed after Tommy's funeral mass," she says. "Tommy's casket sat out in the pouring rain by himself."

When I get back to my car, I'm pissed. I have a headache from all the cigarette smoking going on in the house. The smoke hangs on my clothes. I can smell it on my hands. In the next instant I want a cigarette, although I quit more than seventeen years ago. Worse than that, I'd like a beer. The beers Tom's sisters were drinking on a hot summer afternoon had looked pretty damn good to this boy. If they offered me one right now, I'm not sure I could turn it down.

So what if Tom drank himself to death. There are worse ways to die. Cancer, for one.

This has to end. I'm not getting anywhere. "Tom was a nice guy. He was just fucked up." "Your mother wanted to be a nun, and then she met your father. All she cared about was her family. She had such faith." People die. Deal with it. It's not as if your family were the victims of genocide. Everybody has the same stories. It's like a party line. It's easy to see how myths take root. The person disappears only to reappear as larger yet somehow diminished. Parts of the dead person become the whole.

As I drive away from Ruthanne's house I speed through stop signs, pounding the steering wheel, trying to figure out what's wrong with me, wanting a drink or a joint for the first time in years. A few days after I return from Ruthanne's house, I rip Tom's autopsy into pieces, hoping this symbolic act will put an end to things.

I now hate everything about this. I hate the report. I hate that Tom died. I hate Tom for killing himself. I hate my old friends for not knowing anything about him. I hate his family for loving and judging him. I hate myself for digging around in his death. I hate myself for wanting to drink again. I hate myself for envying Tom.

Tom's overdose has become a magnet. I want to use again. What's the point of any of this?

I need to let it all go. I'm through.

8

I try to get through the fall without any major trouble. Although I haven't been back to the neighborhood and have stopped talking to old friends about days and companions gone by, the ground has shifted beneath me.

The first sign of trouble is the harvest moon. My favorite moon for its constant beauty. But its constant beauty is gone. The moon is now nothing more than a stain in the sky. Will I ever be able to see beauty again? Will anything ever be beautiful again? These are my thoughts. I can't explain them or make them something they're not. I can't fictionalize this moment and make myself bigger or better than I am. I'm nothing more than a man reduced to hate and tears and self-pity, filled with rage and bile and chaos. I look again at the harvest moon.

Just a stain in the sky.

I distract myself throughout the fall by everyday life: home, school, wife, kids. Nothing's working.

Later that fall I get a call from Dave.

"Hey, dick," Dave says when I answer the phone.

I laugh. Almost nobody I know at the university refers to me this way much anymore.

"Hey, did I tell you what my mom said about the dog from the drive-in?"

"Is it still there?" I ask.

"Get this. After we saw it at the drive-in, people saw it going in and out of garages on the street, dragging out mattresses and shit. It seemed like it was everywhere for a few days after we were there, and then it was gone. Just like that."

I'm not sure if Dave sees significance in the dog's behavior. Does he wonder if it's tied to our visit?

I know now that Rick, Dave, and I will remember that dog for the rest of our lives. The image of the dog is the kind of thing that survives even dementia. In one of my great-aunt's final days, almost all she wanted to talk about was her boxer Duke. She had a picture of Duke tacked up behind her bed, right next to the picture of her husband. I'm not saying my aunt had dementia or was even slightly delusional. She knew who I was when I visited, and I knew she loved me. That's a certain kind of clarity as far as I'm concerned. All I'm saying is that perhaps Duke was a drooling flesh-and-blood symbol of a time when life worked just the way it was supposed to work. Duke tapped his nails across the kitchen floor in western Pennsylvania when my aunt was still young enough to hope, still young enough to know only one side of love, still decades away from burying two of her three sons. Through it all, there was Duke. The drive-in dog has just this kind of potential. Not only will he remind us twenty years from now of the January morning in our forties when we tried to pull a piece of our collective past back from the abyss, we'll also recall the black-and-brown boxer (some descendant of Duke's?) because the dog inhabited a place we inhabited in a time when we were so young there was no such thing as a friend's dying in his thirties with nothing, no such thing as thinking that twenty-five years ago was as good as it was going to get for some of us. All of this was flat-out inconceivable then, the stuff of stories not one of us could have imagined.

So the boxer will live on.

Dogs appear to play a big part in the lives of my forgotten Fairlawn friends.

One of my old Fairlawn friends, the Big C – a huge lump of a man who was a good enough bowler to work as a pro for part of his early life – believes his dogs are about all he needs. "I've got my house. I've got my dogs. I'm happy as fuck."

I wonder if all I have to do is add the house and dogs together and I'll understand all that he doesn't have.

At his father's funeral, the Big C stayed out in the parking lot of the funeral home, drinking steadily. He drank until he could face the sight of his father lying dead in a casket. When he did enter the funeral home, he swayed as he made his way to the coffin.

When he reached the coffin he began by removing a pin from the lapel of his father's suit. Then he grabbed his father's right earlobe with his thumb and index finger, and with the pin in the other hand, began trying to pierce his dead dad's ear. I know that the Big C possessed a certain kind of knowledge that day, a knowledge known to the drunk and delusional. The knowledge a guy has when he picks dusk to hurl himself off the Brooklyn Bridge. The truth known to a woman who leaps from her thirtieth-story balcony, blessed and beckoned by the lights of LA.

When his sister saw what was happening, she ran to the coffin.

"Mike, stop it! Leave Daddy alone!" she cried.

"Dad would want this!" the Big C cried out as he continued pushing the pin through his father's earlobe and jerking his arm out of his sister's grasp. "Dad would love this."

Though it no doubt caused his family and friends serious discomfort, perhaps even a little pain, I love the Big C at this moment. I have no doubt he believed, as only a drenched and grieving son can believe, that his deceased father would indeed love to have his ear pierced by a Boy Scout pin he received after years of being a scout leader. And to have that ear pierced by his only son!

I'm quite confident that never before on this planet, or any other, has a son tried to pierce his dead father's ear with a Boy Scout pin. The Big C has earned himself a place in history.

Years after the piercing, he told me that he often visits his dad's grave. When he does, he brings his dogs and let's them run around the cemetery while he drinks with his dad.

"I always bring my dogs and a bottle with me," the Big C said. "I pour a drink for me, and then I pour one on my dad's grave for him. My dad taught me about death."

If I listen carefully, I can hear the booze splashing on the grave-stone – or perhaps the Big C pours it on the surrounding grass so it has a chance to sink into the earth before it evaporates. I can see his dogs sniffing and pissing their way around the cemetery, loving the open lawn, the sturdy trees. And the Big C knows he is never more alive than at moments like this. He understands something when he's here having a drink with his dad. The holiness of being alive reveals itself to him here, and he doesn't retrieve his dogs and walk back to his car until he's been made aware of the rare holiness of his ritual.

When I hear Dave's voice again, I realize I haven't been listening to him.

"What?"

"I said how about around 5:00 or 5:30 Friday, dick?"

"Sounds good."

"It will give me time to take care of the dog after I get home," Dave says. "I have to feed him, take him out. If somebody's here, he won't eat or go out. He'll have to be in your face the whole time."

"What kind of dog do you have now?" I ask.

"Shepherd."

"Cool," I say, lamely.

I pray he doesn't ask me. I'm not sure I could admit to owning – and loving! – a shih tzu named Sophie.

"Friday night will be good," Dave says. "It's my drinking night."

Dave starts to tell me about the altruistic motorcycle club he be-longs to, Rolling Thunder Inc. Along with helping veterans and their families, the club drives around to bars in the area. In each bar they visit they collect a small donation – of money, not booze, although I cannot imagine all of this is done dry – that will go to somebody in need. One time the money went to help pay the medical bills of a young boy with cancer, whose parents had lost their jobs and their health insurance. Another time the money went to help a guy who had lost a foot in an accident of some kind.

I'm stunned that Dave is back on a motorcycle at all. When he was twenty-three he was hit by a truck. He and his Harley wound up beneath the semi; both man and machine were mangled. Dave spent the next six months in bed with broken legs and back.

I cancel this meeting with Dave and several others with him and Rick. Now it's almost Christmas, and I'm in bad shape.

As Christmas closes in, I'm angry, depressed, and feeling sorry for myself. Ever since I can remember, the Christmas season has always depressed the living hell out of me. I like to blame this on my mother's being in her first coma during Christmas, even though my siblings like to remind me that she woke up from that coma on Christmas Eve and spoke to us from the hospital, by phone, on that blessed eve. It was the first time we had heard her voice in days.

But I know my seasonal melancholy began much earlier than my eighteenth year. Even as a child, and especially as an early teen, I expanded my hope and expectations for the yuletide beyond reason. Soon I'd find myself in a state of gloom, moaning because "the season" and so many other earthly things rarely worked out the way I thought they should. This ramping up of the season, of course, is widespread, which did nothing to alleviate my depression. I figured the only way to appreciate Christmas was to have no belief and less hope.

By the time Christmas comes around, and even though I have spent almost two years digging through the past of my neighborhood, picking off every scab, poking at every bruise, the semester ends, and I begin to feel a little better. I feel confident I'll be fine. I feel so fine, in fact, that I agree to meet Rick and Dave, not to talk about Tom but just to chat with two old friends over the holidays. I meet them in a bar, which is not a good idea.

I'm playing with fire now, and I know it.

I arrive at the bar a bit later than Dave and Rick, and they've already begun drinking. I order bottled water and later coffee. I'm sure Rick and Dave have over ten beers each, along with the occasional shot. I see no discernible change in Rick's demeanor, but Dave does seem to be slowly letting loose a more aggressive and aggrieved part of his personality. I have no business spending five hours in a bar. I can get addicted to any substance known to humankind that is likely to change the way I feel from this moment to the next. I haven't spent much time trying to figure out why this is true; I'm kept quite busy, thank you, reminding myself of this in order to stay sober. I realize there has been tremendous research on why one person is easily addicted and another is not, some of the research likely pinning the source on heredity, lack of breast feeding, or being abused as a toddler by a Shetland pony. Although I'm insatiably curious, I've stayed away from trying to discover why.

While we talk and laugh at the bar, bits of Tom's autopsy blow across the bow of my mind. "Self-administered overdose."

The real question is why I'm sitting in a bar for hours. If I'm being honest, I suppose on some level I like being there. I want these guys to drink. I want to reenact old times. I want to drink. Why not?

"Self-administered overdose."

Not a bad way to go, really.

A day or two later, I feel odd, as if some gear had been turned one revolution too far. I'm suddenly calibrated differently. Thoughts of the year my mother suffered and died descend on me like bricks landing on a sparrow. I recall giving her morphine shots and then rushing out into the night to disappear into drugs and alcohol. Despair and reprieve, reprieve and despair; like a mad magician forcing me to pick one hand or the other, I go back and forth between these two worlds, never finding whatever prize existed in either hand.

Autopsy echoes haunt me: "Heart of normal configuration."

Perhaps from a bizarre combination of pathology and weakness, I long to live again in these twin states of despair and reprieve, as if they could possibly hold something for me now, over twenty-five years later. But my reasons for despair now are practically nonexistent. Except that the world we now live in is a frightening mess and our country is becoming less our country with every passing day, on a more personal level I'm content. My wife is smart, successful, loving, beautiful, and the best person I know. I have great kids and work I love. And yet . . . And yet . . .

I know something is missing. Perhaps I haven't really grieved for my mother. Maybe I need to find out more of who she was as a person. And if I'm not finished grieving, Christmas is the best time to reengage the twin dark towers of despair and reprieve, desolation and consolation.

But please, grow the fuck up! Right? If you're saying this as you read, I agree with you. I've said it countless times to myself.

"Heart valves are thin, pliable, delicate."

Still, soon despair has me tight, and my chosen reprieve brings me lower than I've been for over twenty years.

9

The days leading up to Christmas are a blur. For weeks I haven't written a word. I haven't logged a single mile on my bike. Without writing and without exercise, my mood grows darker and darker. Hope of any kind seems the pathetic panacea of fools. When my solipsism abates for a minute, my mind's eye sees my children's future as nothing but a pendulum swinging between entropy and tragedy. I hate waking up. I long for sleep. For weeks, every single morning when my alarm clock rings, I salute the new day with "fuck" or "shit." It's how I say hello to a new morning – "morning . . . excellent and fair," to quote the last line of William Styron's novel *Sophie's Choice*. I soon don't care about following up with Dave and Rick. Tom's death seems nothing but one more meaningless and wasted life ended, hardly worth knowing about, hardly worth the care.

How I have sunk into this mess, I'm not sure. I would love to blame some of this on my country's wanton invasion of Iraq and the overthrow of its sovereign, if despicable, leader. But I know it's something much more personal. Spending all that time on Fairlawn Drive surely shook something loose. I think of Tom's overdose; I'm plagued with thoughts of my mom's too long and too short battle with cancer. I feel the renewed weight of Lisa's father's fatal aneurysm. At some time in the past twenty-five years, I either have stopped grieving or have never stopped grieving for the "beaten and butchered and betrayed and martyred children of the earth," as Styron writes, also at the end of *Sophie's Choice*.

Or, perhaps more correctly, the beaten and butchered and betrayed children of Fairlawn Drive. Those who were beaten by drugs like Tom; butchered by cancer like my mother and three other women her age who all lived within ten houses of each other; the blue-collar men betrayed by the American dream and the faith of their fathers.

Or perhaps the only person I ever mourned was myself, the man I thought I'd be, the person I wanted to become.

In a world filled with hatred and violence, warfare and genocide, tears for the person next door can feel small indeed; but they don't. I wish that knowledge of all the earth's misery did, somehow, dwarf my own sadness. But it doesn't. It only adds to it.

Ultimately, of course, I have no one but myself to blame for what is about to happen.

Nothing appears on the horizon of winter but darkness. Although I've never really enjoyed winter, this year I begin to loathe it. Its early nights, its unending snow and cold. I'm ashamed that a season could knock me so far off my stride, but that's what's happening.

As we've done every winter for the past fifteen years, my wife, our two daughters, and I drive to Missouri to visit my in-laws for the Christmas holidays. My son stays with his mother and her family for Christmas; all five of us have our own celebration, complete with a makeshift Christmas morning, a week or so before the actual day. My mother-in-law, at eighty-three, still prepares feasts for the holidays. My sister- and brother-in-law, our niece and her husband, our nephew and his wife, all meet in Missouri for a country Christmas. Holiday distractions abound.

This Christmas nothing helps. I've been in a renewed depression since a week after Thanksgiving. So for the first time in fifteen years, I decide I need a little help getting through the holidays. Doing any drinking or illicit drugs is not an option. Things are not that bad, I tell myself. What I need is some kind of pain relief. Yeah, that's it. Relief from pain. A painkiller.

For the past several years I've been afflicted with a pain in the ass, quite literally. On long drives, or after hours in hard chairs, my coccyx begins to ache.

So I get on the Internet, the worldwide drugstore. After some light research, I settle on the painkiller tramadol, a generic version of Ultram, prescribed primarily for joint pain. Not exactly heroin, but it will have to do. I start taking two or three a day. I don't give a damn about my coccyx, but I'm sure as hell happy for the slight change in my state of mind, that opaque numbness, that shroud of mist that fogs reality. I swallow as many as I can with blatant abandon.

"Self-administered overdose."

As always in my relationship with mood-altering substances, the good moments are brief and fleeting and are soon followed, in the time-honored pattern, by the bitter misery of trying to feel better by taking more, and more.

I've been using tramadol for weeks by the time we go to Missouri. As hard as I try, I can recall practically nothing from our Christmas visit there. I'm sure I engaged in the requisite small talk and wore a forced smile during gift giving and meals. The only other events I remember are a visit to my wife's aunt in the nursing home and my desperate sortie to the library to hook in to the electronic pharmacy.

The nursing home fits my mood perfectly. Dandi's aunt Dot is eighty-eight, independent and strong. She also has an amazing past. As a nurse in World War II, she married in the Philippines during the war. In the way of many quick war marriages, duty and orders separated Dot and her new husband, Emanuel "Boots" Engel Jr. Shortly thereafter the Japanese overran the islands. Dot and other nurses hid in the jungle, eating anything they could find, including native monkeys. In 1942 Aunt Dot and a handful of other nurses escaped Corregidor and were the first American women decorated for bravery in World War II. But Dot's husband was killed on an enemy transport ship in 1944. For years after the war ended, Dot continued to search for his name on lists of survivors until, "[I] came to see that he was never coming home." After being the subject of many articles and of the movie *So Proudly We Hail* (Aunt Dot being portrayed by Claudette Colbert), and after being hosted and celebrated by Eleanor Roosevelt, Dot returned to the small Missouri town she grew up in. She worked for her doctor brother alongside her sister-in-law – my mother-in-law – also a nurse. When she stopped working she spent a great deal of her time playing bingo and smoking, alone with her cats in a house slowly closing in on her. She'd fill a room with papers and keepsakes and heirlooms until that room was unlivable, then she'd close it off and move into another. When only one room was left and she could no longer take care of herself as she had for the past sixty years, she entered the nearby veterans' nursing home, where we found her this Christmas.

All the usual suspects can be found in this nursing home. Geriatrics, some missing limbs, others missing minds, sit or lie among foot-high fake Christmas trees and beneath tacky, too-bright red-and-green garlands. All these people have suffered thousands times more than I could ever imagine, yet I walk in with my own small baggage, wanting nothing more than to leave. My wife and I visit Dot for a while. We talk briefly, then walk her out to our car to bring her to the family Christmas.

For a brief moment I feel a twinge of real life. It comes when I carry Aunt Dot's purse for her and hold her arm to steady her gait. That feels real to me. I have participated in an actual moment.

Despite my one true moment, the nursing home fills me with despair and confirms all my suspicions. No matter how you live your life, if you sacrifice years, limbs, even sanity for a cause greater than yourself, if you hide in the jungle and eat monkeys to preserve your precious life, if you're the subject of a movie and are hosted by a great first lady and decorated by the Red Cross, you'll wind up neglected by caretakers, living with ailing strangers, all in their last days, mumbling and bumbling, drooling and stooling, unable to feed yourself or incontinent or both, and some lucky middle-aged asshole who's depressed and drugged will walk through the place with his beautiful wife and make judgments about the quality of your existence while he's whining about his own.

The only other moment I can recall occurs in the library of a nearby town, open on the day after Christmas. I log on and begin ordering. I want to use up the pills I've brought. I'm convinced I'll never make it through the visit without them. So I order two more bottles of tramadol to be delivered to the university mailroom when we return home the following Saturday. With the order successfully placed, I drive back to my mother-in-law's place, content at least that my supply appears safe. I stay pretty much numb for the rest of the visit, not all that different from everybody else's food-filled holiday stupor.

When we get home, I rush to the university, only to find the mailroom closed and the place deserted. I call security and tell the officer on duty that I have an important FedEx package in the mailroom – my "medicine," I inform him – and I need to get in there right away. The officer complies, but when he comes out of the mailroom he's empty-handed. No drugs.

"Are you sure?" I ask. "Would you mind checking again?"

He does. Still no drugs.

With the nearest FedEx office closed on the weekend, I spend sleepless white nights Saturday and Sunday, thrashing around in bed. First thing Monday morning I drive to FedEx. Apparently, because the mailroom was closed, the drugs went back on the FedEx truck to be delivered that Monday or Tuesday. Because the university gives its employees the week between Christmas and New Year's off, no delivery could be made, and the drugs went back to some FedEx holding station, leaving me drug-addled and pissed.

After only a month on the drug, I spend hours driving around, listening to Christmas music and sobbing like an abandoned child. That Tuesday, the final Tuesday of the year, I drive around endlessly, listening over and over to the Vince Guaraldi Trio singing the fucking Charlie Brown Christmas song, "Christmas Time Is Here." The trio's angelic voices sing of beauty and joy everywhere, while I drive and sob and play the two minute-and-forty-four-second song over and over again, as if they are the only minutes of music available to me, looking for beauty, longing for joy.

This is not Mozart's *Requiem*, for Chrissake! And yet, to me, on this endlessly cold day filled with dirty snow, shaking with rage, rattled by depression, wanting nothing more than to feel hope, the fucking Charlie Brown Christmas song brings me lower than any piece of music ever has. To know on an intellectual level that beauty and joy and goodness and happiness are available to me and yet not be able to produce a gnat-sized hint of the actual feelings is almost more than I can stand.

After my tear-stained ride, I do what any self-respecting addict who knows he has hit bottom does – I hurry home and order more drugs.

10

In January, Dandi starts keeping her distance, not wanting to be sucked into the vortex of my selfish madness. I'm such a mess by this time that I don't even realize this is happening. I want nothing more than for school to begin, I tell myself. Surely teaching my classes and keeping busy with editing and meetings and committees will help me regain my waning sanity.

At the end of the first week of school, I want nothing more than to leave the university. I need time off, even though I've just had a month, more vacation than some people accrue all year. If people would just leave me alone, I'd be okay. If my students weren't all so goddamn needy, I'd have some time to take care of myself.

My selfishness knows no bounds.

Whenever I'm down to thirty-odd pills, I log on to the Internet and order more drugs. Next-day delivery by FedEx. The FedEx guy practically knows me by name. I have the drugs shipped to the university mailroom so I can keep my addiction secret from my family.

At the same time, I know that to end the chemical chaos all I need do is to tell my wife, or a friend, or my doctor the truth, and I could begin climbing out of this black pit. But as much as I tell myself I want to quit, I keep the secret and continue buying the drugs.

Hell, it's not even really a narcotic, I tell myself. It's not codeine or Vicodin. I'm okay. Through the weeks that follow I'm prepared to tell the people in the mailroom that I'm taking diet pills, which are obviously not working, or even Viagra, which surely is working, which is why I'm receiving so many FedEx deliveries.

At the end of January I order several bottles, one each from different online businesses. I have to prepare myself for February, surely the cruelest month, despite T. S. Eliot's wasted sentiments about April. February is also the most honest of months in my part of the country. One can count on February to be cold and snowy and dark and desolate, its dim days crawling toward the vastly dishonest yet hoped-for March with all the speed and urgency of my long-ago forced processions through the incense-choked Stations of the Cross with a priest and his penitents.

And so I stock up. I stockpile nearly three hundred, surely enough for February. When spring comes I can start riding my bike and weaning myself off the pills. These will be the last I'll have to buy.

Soon I have only thirty or so, with still three weeks of February to go. Each night before bed, I convince myself I've taken my last pill, that I'll confide in Dandi and seek help. I'll stop living a lie as a hypocrite and a fraud. Each morning I take the pledge of abstinence. Each afternoon the cycle begins anew.

Swearing off the pills during the school day, which I congratulate myself for doing, I simply shorten my day by leaving campus immediately after my last class. The moment I get home, sequestering myself in my office under the guise of work that has to be done, I work for maybe an hour before I begin my nightly mindless vigil of staring at the television.

After doing her own writing for nearly twelve hours, Dandi joins me at eight or nine o'clock for an hour of a quasi-watchable drama, and then I go to sleep. And so the days pass.

Occasionally I get a call from Dave or Rick asking when we can get together and what else I want to know about Tom. When I call back, it's weakly and without interest. I tell my old friends I'm just busy with school and that we'll get together soon.

Whenever I'm alone, I wind up in a cocoon of sadness and self-pity, crying over I don't know what. No matter how miserable addicts get, asking for help is the one outward sign of weakness that they, we, at least I, cannot abide. While only I know of my gargantuan weakness, I can wallow in it. So I do not tell my wife or my family or my friends or my doctors. I don't ask for help, because that would mean I'd be admitting weakness.

Plus, asking for help would mean I'd have to quit.

I know I couldn't face a day of life on life's terms, as those in recovery like to say. So I buy more. Buying on the Internet is shockingly easy. Typing in a credit card number, filling out a brainless questionnaire, and capitalizing on somebody else's greed are all that's necessary. And buy I do.

While I'm of my own mind and in the classroom, I give the hour or two everything I can, which I'm sure is not enough. Classes, which are usually invigorating, exhaust me. Because I have a reputation as a good and caring teacher, an active scholar, and because I'm a tenured professor willing to serve on committees, I know I can coast for a semester without anybody's noticing.

At least I hope so.

Every faculty meeting goes on far too long. Every bit of work I have to do seems monumentally difficult. What's the point anyway? Who cares what any of us plans or what work any of us does when we're just going to disappear and die in the meaningless mayhem of the early twenty-first century?

There are times I wish a friend, colleague, or student would walk into my office and say that I don't seem to be myself lately, would sit down and ask me what's wrong. In my wishfulness, I imagine telling everything. But I doubt if even that kind of intervention could save me.

I know now what a mistake going back "home" has been. Fuck it all. None of it matters. Tom was a loser. My mother should have gone to a doctor earlier. I blame her blind Catholicism and the church's divine fear of all things sexual for my assertion that she delayed telling anyone or seeing a doctor because the cancer had shown up in her breast. If the disease had manifested itself on her skin or her tongue, she likely would have sought medical help immediately.

Anyway, that was so long ago. Everybody else has moved on. Why can't I?

After I restock for February, I think I see the end of this new addiction. All I need to do is get through the winter. But by mid-February I've lost sight of any hope. Spring will be no different from winter. More sunlight and warmer weather cannot possibly cure what ails me. What that is, I still don't know. Are depression and drugs the chicken or the egg?

February 14 arrives, a Saturday. Valentine's Day. Without planning it until I wake up that morning, I tell my wife I'm going to visit my mother's two older sisters. After all, I'm sure they'll like to see their nephew on this, the twenty-fifth anniversary of his mother's, their sister's, death.

Not wanting to arrive without gifts, I stop at a local candy store famous for its chocolate-covered strawberries. I choose the branch on Brookpark Road in Cleveland, just across from Holy Cross Cemetery. I buy two boxes of the strawberries and drive up toward West 150th, wanting to drive to my aunt's house by the same route we took when I was a kid.

But first . . .

First I pull into the cemetery and start trying to find my mother's grave. I know I can find its general location, because I still remember a landmark or two. Finding her specific stone will be a lot harder. Maybe all I need is a good cry at my mother's grave.

Pulling to the side of the road and getting out of the car, I begin my search. Snow covers nearly all the stones in the vicinity. I walk away from my car and spot the Dairy Queen in the deep distance, which I've used as my landmark in the past. What my relation to the landmark is supposed to be, I can't remember. I'm not somebody who thinks in terms of something's being a forty-five-degree angle from the east side of the Dairy Queen. My search is more intuitive. Does it feel as if this is where I stood to look down on my mother's stone and offer up a prayer I once believed had power? That's my approach. And it's not working well. I've kicked the snow off so many stones bearing the names of other dead mothers, husbands, and kids that I want to quit.

Hell, what's the real point of finding the exact stone? It's not as if she's really under there. I know parts of her body are there, but she is not. I understand the power of symbols. . . . But if she's not there, where is she? My belief system really doesn't account for her "spirit," except as it exists in the minds and hearts of those who loved her, in the stories told, and in the memories stored.

However, not having stood over my mother's stone in too many years to count, I can't leave without finding the damn thing. As a former journalist, I pride myself on being able to discover latent facts and to locate places, people, and information a lot of other people cannot. Even in my drugged and depressed state, I have to find the stone.

I mentally map out a section of the grass where I decide it must be, and then I pace up every snowy aisle, clearing enough of the stones for me to count them out. While I do this I can't resist looking to see how long people have lived. I love stones where the dead lived seventy, eighty, ninety years. The next second I'm pissed that my mother didn't live to see her forty-fifth birthday.

Now I'm forty-five. How could I have outlived her?

While I search I long to hear the antidirge of the cemetery's resident geese, but they're as silent as the snow.

And then, moving over just a little farther than I think it can be, I see the name Christine, and I know it's her.

CHRISTINE MACKALL, MOTHER, 1934–1979."

I stare down at her stone, look up, gaze around. Having sobbed for hours not too long ago while listening to a cartoon hymn, I'm prepared for a gush of authentic emotion while standing at the foot of my mother's grave a quarter of a century after her death. Valentine's Day, after all. I feel nothing except relief.

There. See, I'm fine. I no longer need to grieve. It's over. I walk to my car.

I understand that I no longer have an authentic bone in my body. Authenticity must have gone the way of innocence and faith. And once they're gone, there's no getting them back, is there?

What I remember from the day my mother died was that I was in my sophomore year of college at Cleveland State University, taking a geology test. How the test went, I have no recollection.

After the bus, then train, then bus ride home, I was dropped off at the corner of the street, just three blocks from St. Bees and six blocks from home. On the bus I had spent the ride watching the water from thawing boots carry trash in its tiny current, flowing toward the driver when he braked and back to the passengers when the bus lurched forward. These city buses were little Clevelands: dirty, past their prime, smelly and noisy, crowded with disappointment and anger, but still having the fuel to move forward.

The snow fell fat and steady as I walked home from the bus stop that day. Suddenly I saw a young girl, in her teens perhaps, walking toward me, still several blocks away. When I got closer I could see that it was my sister Ann. What was she doing walking up Queens Highway in the middle of the afternoon? Why wasn't she in school? Even though I knew my mother would die any day now, my mind wouldn't let me imagine, at that moment, that what I had feared for the past year and a half had indeed occurred that morning, while I took a geology test.

Ann walked up to me. She hugged me and said, "Mom died." We walked the few blocks home as the snow fell.

I was the only family member not in the hospital with her the morning she died.

When Ann and I arrived home, the house was already filled with family, friends, and food. The hugs were welcome, the coffee warm.

All I wanted to do was hang on until nine that night, when I'd be able to hide away in my room and watch *Julius Caesar* on PBS. I knew I could be transported on the wings of William Shakespeare, beautifully dramatizing lives and deaths, and that this would help me feel catharsis rather than mere sadness, pathos rather than pity. I hung on until nine o'clock.

It was that night that I, at least on some subconscious level, shifted my faith from Catholicism to literature.

The night of my mother's death was not the first time I understood the saving power of literature.

During the final days of the "before" of my life on Fairlawn Drive, I would wake up, walk upstairs from my basement bedroom, light a cigarette, pour a cup of coffee, grab a syringe, and poke a morphine-wet needle through the orange-peel feel of my mother's skin, a skin becoming nothing more than a taut shroud covering a body succumbing to the chaos of cancer. After saying good-bye to Mom, Dad, and whoever else was around on those days – sometimes a visiting nurse, a family friend, or a parish priest – I'd leave the house and all the doom it seemed to hold.

But one day turned out differently, thanks to a story. My routine began the same: morphine shot for Mother, a joint for me, bus, then train, then bus ride to one more day of university life.

By the time I sat down in Professor Hazelrig's English 102 class, my pot buzz was gone and my life was about to change. Hazelrig had assigned a reading that apparently few in the class had read, so he gave us the first quarter of the class to read the story – which I had read; reading and writing were about the only work I did in those early college years. By the time I finished reading the story for the fifth or sixth time in twenty-four hours – J. D. Salinger's "A Perfect Day for Bananafish" from the collection *Nine Stories*, I was hopeful, actually felt hope, that not everything was death, dying, disease, and despair.

In Salinger's story, minutes before the protagonist, Seymour Glass, kills himself in his Florida hotel room while his wife sleeps on the next bed, he encounters a little girl named Sybil on the beach. As Seymour talks to Sybil, he explains to her the dangers of becoming a bananafish. "What's a bananafish?" Sybil asks. He tells her that bananafish live at the bottom of the ocean, where they burrow into holes in search of food, and then they eat and eat and eat until they fill the hole and can't get out. They get trapped, and then they die. They have become the hole. When Seymour finishes his lesson on the doomed fish, Sybil looks out at the ocean, squints, points, and then exclaims that she thinks she sees one.

At that moment, sitting in the back of the room in a leather jacket and the fog of fatalism, I believed Sybil was pointing at me. Thanks to Sybil, Seymour, and Salinger, I realized I had entered a hole that I hadn't truly seen. My hole was a mother's cancer and impending death, a family with a splitting nucleus, and one angry, confused, dulled-by-dope nineteen-year-old sitting in English class. But somehow, on some level, after the day with the bananafish, I realized that another door had opened to me. Perhaps it was my Catholic upbringing to see salvation in a fish, but I knew then that stories had the power to change lives, even to save them, and that literature could become my new church.

(A footnote to the bananafish story: Needing a letter of recommendation for a graduate teaching assistantship in English, I called Professor Hazelrig ten years after my epiphanic moment with a fish in his class. As we talked I remembered the way he taught the Salinger story that day: the way he nearly shivered while he talked about it, the way he seemed to feel the power of story and literature. He understood that it was life and death. But the day we spoke about my letter of recommendation, he sounded listless and tired. When I asked how things were going, he told me he was having a rough time as the executor of his brother's estate. His brother had killed himself with a bullet to the brain. The modus operandi of Seymour Glass. Another "perfect day for bananafish.")

My last couple of college years were nothing but drinking, reading, having fun, trying to forget. My friends and I spent a great deal of time in the Shire, the bar in the basement of Cleveland State University's student center. We wasted – and I mean wasted – entire days in the Shire. On Fridays in particular, several of us would drive to school together, get high on the way there, blow off our classes, and wait for the Shire to open.

(It never struck me as odd that nearly all my close friends from Fairlawn Drive went to our local university. There was no talk of going away to college. Our parents had no money. Student loans were available. Cleveland State was cheap. What's there to think about? What's there to dream about?)

What I didn't know until years later was that during the times I knew I was figuratively building my life on and off the working-class world of my father and men like him, I was doing it literally as well. When a thirty-eight-year-old electrician was wiring Cleveland State University to prepare it for me to write, read, think, and drink in, a large bolt fell hundreds of feet and landed on his head, killing him instantly. He left behind a wife, two sons, and a daughter. His younger son, only thirteen at the time, would marry my sister Ann.

My friends and I would start drinking under the university's bright lights at ten on Friday morning, drink until four or five o'clock, drive home, "shit, shower, and shave," then head back downtown for a party Friday night. The downtown regulars referred to us as the suburban wrecking crew.

On one Shire-drenched day just before I graduated – drunk, but also drunk on the saving grace of literature and wanting to tell the world – I ran from one empty classroom to another belting out a paean to the world's great writers. I scrawled the names Dostoevsky and Hemingway and Ellison and Whitman and Keats, and Fitzgerald and Hardy and Shakespeare and Milton, and George Eliot and Margaret Atwood and Mary Shelley, and Baldwin, Updike, and Styron. Chalk cracked in my hand as I wrote dusty hymns to the priests and priestesses of my education.

With a beer in one hand, I chalked my favorite Thomas De Quincy quotation from memory: "And of this let everyone be assured – that he owes to the impassioned books which he has read many a thousand more that he can consciously trace back to them . . . these emotions yet arise in him, and mould him through life, like forgotten incidents of his childhood." Literature ruled my life. I consulted it for advice. I sought its moral guidance. I worshipped in its riotous quietude.

Twenty-one and a senior in college, I was engaged. Mary is the best woman I have ever known except for my wife. She deserved better. I thought I loved her as much as any wild, immature, twenty-one-year-old dreamer can love a woman. Mary came from a white-collar family where lawyers abounded. I saw myself as her blue-collar project, a guy with lots of potential, though rough as hell around the edges. Plus, Mary considered herself a bit of a rebel. She was the youngest child and the only girl. She was smart, funny, pretty, sexy, good.

Through her father's connections, I was interviewed and landed a job as a management trainee in the J. C. Penney organization. Mary was delighted. Now we could be married in three months, and we'd be able to support ourselves. We found a nice little house to rent. Mary began fixing up the house as I finished school. Graduating in a recession with an English degree, even I found some solace in having a job lined up for after graduation.

But soon I got antsy. Hell, petrified. How could I possibly get married now? I'd only be twenty-two! What about writing? What about literature? One woman for the rest of my life? What does a management trainee do anyway?

At the time I was reading John Fowles's amazing novel *The French Lieutenant's Woman*. In Fowles's 1969 take on Victorian novels and the Victorian mores and sensibilities he still saw at work in the late sixties, his protagonist, Charles, has been set up in a business he despises by Mr. Freeman, the father of his intended, Ernestina. Not long before the marriage is to take place, Charles meets Sarah, the French lieutenant's woman, and realizes he's about to embark on a life he has no interest in living. He understands that he is "in suspension between the two worlds, the warm, neat civilization behind his back, the cool, dark mystery outside."

An unmarried future as a single writer was my "cool, dark mystery."

Sarah was the only person in the novel who was completely free. She had rejected Victorian conventions, including marriage, religion, virtue, even the truth. Although she was a virgin until her first time with Charles, the town considered her a whore, and she let the lie stand. She stood alone and free, an emancipation won by rejection.

Nearly every parallel hit home. For months I had been thinking about breaking off the engagement, but I believed it was too late. After all, we had a house and the hall and had sent out invitations, and Mary had a ring and I had a job and our family and friends were happy for us. Ending it was impossible.

But what about Charles? What about Sarah? I saw in myself the truth I saw in the character of Charles. My destiny was clear. I had to break it off.

Two months before the wedding, Mary surprised me one Sunday morning by stopping by my house. She found me behind the garage, smoking a joint, looking hangdog and miserable.

"What are you doing?" she asked. "Why are you getting high on a Sunday morning?"

"I'm not ready to get married," I said.

"The wedding's not for two whole months."

"No. I mean I'm not ready to get married in two months or two years. I'm sorry."

Within minutes we each had a meltdown. We both cried, Mary in anger and sadness, I in stupefaction and sadness. I don't remember much, but I do know that Mary threw her engagement ring at me. It sailed over my head, but it was a nice try. If it had hit me square in the eye, knocking pupil, retina, and cornea to the ground to be chewed, swallowed, and regurgitated by squirrels and other rodents, I would have deserved no better.

For months I joked to all who asked that I had gotten disengaged. I loved the wordplay.

I missed Mary. I knew that I young-loved her and that we would never be together. I took the job at Penney's. One day I spotted a purple summer dress in women's sportswear that was identical to one Mary wore. I ran to the stockroom to hide my eyes. I quit Penney's the next day.

I turn from my mother's grave, get back in my car, and start the engine. As the car warms up, I look around. I can't deny the beauty in this snowbound cemetery. I can't deny that I was borne up by the stories told by the people in these graves. I can't deny that I have to begin carrying the stories with me, so I can leave all the death behind.

When I was a kid, I believed that the children of my grandparents lived the richest and most extraordinary lives anyone has ever lived. But my beliefs were based not on the facts of their lives but on the stories.

Characters with names like Louie the Goose and Two Gun populated the old neighborhood. Not only were the Goose and the Gun given new life through my grandmother's stories, but she also had the ability to transmute her own flesh and blood into memorable characters in the drama called "The Old Neighborhood."

Besides the old neighborhood stories, she had a World War II repertoire, which concentrated not on the horrors or heroics of the battlefield but rather on the nuances of the home front. She had four sons in the war, which I believe gave her the necessary credibility to tell war stories, an honor awarded only a few, albeit a few too many.

One of my uncles spent the war in the belly of a gunner. At seventeen years old he flew ninety missions in six months, one every other day. Not until seven years after the war was he able to surrender the postwar booze and the fight, and his transformation into an upstanding citizen has something to do with a Christmas tree falling on him late one Christmas Eve or early Christmas morning. I learned something important about storytelling from the Christmas tree tale: sometimes bits and pieces of a story become the whole.

One of my all-time favorite war stories is the one about the day her oldest son returned from overseas, ostensibly unharmed. An odd breeze cut through the Cleveland streets that day; as if natural weather patterns were confused, the wind dipped and dived, blowing first one way and then another, spinning newspapers aloft and then hurling them flat against fences, only to let them drop to the ground. In one version of the story, it rained on one side of the street but not the other. While she watched and listened to the wind, a knock came at the door. "Do you have any food for a hungry soldier?" As mother and son hugged, hugs designed to help close the void of four years and soothe the scars of separation, the soldier's boots shuffled on the wooden porch on the day the wind seemed possessed.

I heard this story for the first time the week of my tenth birthday, the week I decided I hated war and loved wooden porches. Now I have a wooden porch. Now I have a son.

On VE Day women and their daughters, old men and young boys took to the streets of Cleveland, banging pots and pans in a raucous domestic parade of thanks. I'm told the clanging could be heard for hours and for miles.

The family stories come in a flood. When I think they're finished with me, I find there's one more, the last story my maternal grandmother ever told me. I heard it at Christmastime over a decade ago, when my brother and I went to visit her, bringing flowers, eggs, and milk, partly because we wanted to shower her with gifts, partly because we knew we didn't visit her often enough. The smell of the coffee brewed at five that morning permeated the air, filling the house with a comforting familial warmth. I noticed a small bandage covering a missing chip of paint on the stove.

She began telling us something several of her great-grandchildren had done some time ago. And then, right in the middle of that story, mingled naturally with the children she spoke of, she talked about how, while her great-grandchildren played in the yard, they were joined by her youngest child, our mother. My brother and I looked at each other, smiled, and looked away. The furnace kicked on, embracing us in an abrupt warmth.

Our mother had been dead for over twelve years. She never met these particular great-grandchildren, having died long before they were born. But for my grandmother, her daughter danced and played under the pine tree in the front yard with children from another time.

As I sit in this cemetery, I try to imagine my mother and my children running beneath the pine tree, twirling around its trunk until they grow dizzy with the energy and promise of a childhood summer. Their laughter fills the streets. I imagine Tom rising up out of a car on a hot August afternoon, uniting with his son, finding some kind of dream hidden way down inside him.

For that moment I understand that my grandmother obtained the perfect mix of memory, imagination, and desire. Perhaps all her stories contained this particular mix. Maybe the pots and pans of VE Day weren't all that loud and didn't last quite that long. Maybe the wind blew only westerly and it rained on both sides of the street. Maybe Frankie Yale was nothing more than the Executioner.

Some might say that this passing down of stories from one generation to the next can become a perverse and even dangerous romanticism. One need only think of babies dressed in the garb of the KKK to know this is true. How many children are now being told that the Holocaust never happened?

But what I believe my grandmother really passed on is the hope that things could have been this way, could be this way. Maybe these stories, the beautiful and the dangerous, teach us that it's a matter of vision.

Maybe my vision has been far too dark for far too long. Maybe it's finally caught up with me.

Maybe it's too late for me.

As I leave my mother's grave and drive toward the cemetery's exit, I stop at the geese pond, hoping that perhaps the birds will grant me a little solace. In the foreground of the pond is a sign, written in red and black: "This property is maintained as a Catholic cemetery for the internment, burial and memorialization of the deceased. *Uneven ground, depressions* caused by the settling of loose dirt in graves and general ground conditions create *potential hazards* when walking through the cemetery. When loose dirt is combined with any precipitation, it will become mud and will *not support the weight of a person. Graves* may contain mud and *sinking into the mud is possible.*" Italics all mine.

Yeah, no shit. I get it.

Grateful for seeing the geese near the front cross, I speed out of the cemetery on the quarter-century anniversary of my mother's death, wanting to drive somewhere – not to my aunt's house, not back home, but full speed, pedal to the metal, flat the fuck out, all the way back to the past.

11

February trudges on, as it must.

Arriving at school each morning about nine or ten, I close my office door and hide out. Sometimes I try to write. Sometimes I make futile attempts at garnering enough focus to read. What I feel more than anything is Camus's "wild longing for clarity."

More often than not I just sit, looking for a way out, trying to will the arrival of spring break, when I can be depressed and sorry for myself and selfish and not have to worry about anybody else's needs. My son will be with his mother; my wife and daughters will be visiting my mother-in-law. I'll be able to sit at home and wallow in my own shit. I even resent having to take care of the dog.

While teaching my writing classes, I notice a distinct lack of patience. No patience for tardiness, or absences, or complaints, not even for suggestions or compromises. People who produce poor work are told not only why their writing's poor, but what they need to do to make it better. And I don't mean writing suggestions. I tell people to start caring more about themselves and their colleagues. Life is short. I tell them to pay homage to language and literature with their work instead of taking the easy way out, instead of expecting perfection with every word they write or, worse, believing that what they wrote is perfect and nobody would ever be able to tell them different. Although these professorial rants are not necessarily sinful in themselves, my tone and attitude conspire to make the remarks mean-spirited, something I've never been in or out of a classroom. I could always be an asshole, for sure, but I've never *tried* to be mean. But now I'm ashamed to say that although I don't try to be mean, I don't care if I am, either.

All I want to do is end class, drive home, pop my pills, and mentally meander through the myths of my life.

Besides, how many of these students will really pursue writing as a career? How many will even read a book after they graduate? What does it matter anyway?

I know some people live with these questions their entire lives. I don't understand how they go on. Other people, perhaps the vast majority, can't understand anybody's even having thoughts like these. Life is precious, asshole. Pick yourself up by your bootstraps and get going. Or the really annoying folks will talk about accepting Jesus. Accept Jesus and your drug problem will disappear; all the deaths you've known will be in perfect perspective. You can amuse yourself by tallying which of your dead have been saved and which are rotting in hell. That should keep your mind off your own problems and on Jesus. Or rub the Buddha's belly and inhale the serenity of the East, where problems drift away because they weren't problems in the first place.

I know in my heart it's too late for this. The people who constantly talk about Jesus, particularly those who appear as media heads for all things Christian, are some of the scariest people I know. And the ones who push Buddhism or Hinduism or Judaism or Rastafarianism or New Age holism are nearly as bad.

But I know I'm not being fair. When you're in a hole and have become a bananafish, your vision is vexed by looking up at everybody else from the absolute bottom. And because everybody else is above you, you have to bring them down.

I spend the rest of February doing as little as possible and complaining about how much I have to do. Everything suffers. I begin avoiding people: family, friends, colleagues, students. If I spot students walking across the parking lot or the quad, I pretend I haven't seen them. I know if we talk I'll be forced to do something: answer a question, sign a slip of paper, promise a seat in class, listen to complaints about too much work and too little time, engage another human being in the exquisitely painful act of living.

There's nothing uglier than a bitter middle-aged man.

Just please let me get to spring break and I'll be okay. Whom I beseech, I have no idea.

When the last week before break finally arrives, I'm barely conscious. I slouch toward the week off. Every request is met with "We'll take care of it after spring break." Ironically, I'm also nominated for a prestigious teaching award at the university. Any other time I would have felt honored and welcomed the opportunity to strut my stuff in submitting the material required from all nominees. This just seems like one more chore. And how can I possibly accept this award with a straight face? I'm in the middle of the worst and most ignominious semester of my teaching career; the idea that I may receive an award seems sick, puny, and pathetic. Don't these people know anything? Don't they see what kind of person I am?

And then, when I feel as detached from my life as I've ever been, I contract the "perfect storm" of flu strains. By the Thursday afternoon before spring break, I sit in my university office talking with a young undergraduate about a book of nonfiction she's writing, trying desperately to stay alert and to do her some good. I succeed at the first, barely, and fail, I'm quite sure, at the second.

I leave campus the first second I can. My head aches, I'm nauseated. Chills envelop me one minute and fever the next. It's as if anger, depression, and despair have metamorphosed into flu symptoms. I miss the next day of classes, the last day before break, and by Friday night I'm possessed of the flu, fever, and fucks. My wife and daughters have left for Missouri, and my son's staying with his mother, so the flu runs off with my body and a wickedly virulent strain of the heebie-jeebies feasts on my mind.

My imagination has always been a cunning, uncontrollable vehicle, and for the next forty-eight hours it takes me on a wild ride. Sleeping only seconds at a time, I slip into plots of movies and books, my old friends playing parts I don't recognize them in, while my body shakes and jerks. I have visions of Tom plunging into oblivion amid exhaust fumes and pot smoke. I see myself plunging down behind him. I see my mother in the ground, tears seeping out of her decaying bones as she cries for a cousin dying over and over in a thousand hells. It's as if something has come loose. Neurons explode. Synapses collapse with images of violence.

I must be dying, I think. This must be what it feels like to die. No control over my body. Even less over my mind.

This has to be the end.

For the first time in years, I feel the mad urge to pray. I resist the urge.

By Saturday afternoon, fearing I'll be dead within hours, I muster enough energy to collect all my drugs, throw them in the trash, and drive the trash up to the Dumpster. I sure as hell don't want my wife and children discovering ugly remnants of my secret self after my ignominious death.

The snow is blindingly white. I can barely keep my eyes open. I get to the Dumpster, collect my strength, throw the trash bag in, and hit the compact button, just in case I'm well enough later to entertain the lunatic notion of Dumpster diving to retrieve my drugs. The drive exhausts me. I can't get out of my car. I give it all I have. I sit in the car, in the garage, for first five, then fifteen, then thirty minutes, desperate to get back in bed, afraid to move an inch. It takes me almost forty-five minutes to move.

I never make it back to my bed. I curl up on the bathroom floor, as spastic as Billy Pilgrim, hanging over the toilet and throwing up only water every few minutes for hours and hours. I also regurgitate some psychedelic-looking parts of my body that must have lain dormant and undisturbed for twenty years.

I wake up constantly through the night, wanting it all to end.

I'm still not sure what I mean by "it."

Although I fail to comprehend the extent of my illness, by Sunday morning I'm extremely dehydrated. My mind seething with fevered and ridiculous images where every attempt at clear and rational thought burns through to the next disturbing image like a blowtorch through Kleenex, I phone my wife. Besides being the smartest person I know, Dandi is also the daughter of a doctor and a nurse, which is exactly the kind of help I need. She need not have been a doctor's daughter to know what to do, of course; any clear-thinking six-year-old of either sex would have said basically the same thing. I paraphrase: "Go to the hospital, dumb ass!"

The thought of driving myself to the hospital is enough to make me not go at all. Most of my friends and family either are out of town or live a good distance away.

"Call Dan," my wife insists. "Don't drive yourself. Please."

I don't want to bother my son. He doesn't need to see me this way. I might frighten him, I think. I'm about to call a cab when my wife rings back, insisting I call Dan.

I understand that no matter what Dan's doing, he'll drop everything to come over, which is part of the reason I don't want to call. Plus, armed with the moral ammunition of not having had a drink or an illicit drug for over fifteen years, I'd lectured him often on the dangers of drinking and drugs.

I'm not sure I can face him as the liar and hypocrite I've become in the past few months.

Not long after I talk to my wife for the third or fourth time that morning, I phone Dan, who at nearly twenty-one has been out late the night before and is worshipping at the sacred heart of Saint Mattress.

All I remember about the drive to the hospital is that I drove and my son read the sports pages.

When we get to the emergency room, Dan spots a new-looking vw bug with a fake rose next to the gearshift.

"Oh, that's a girl's car," he says. "If she's cute, I'll sit next to her in the waiting room. Okay?"

I thank him for his constant concern and devotion as we enter Ashland's Samaritan Hospital, a place you ordinarily wouldn't take a broken pinkie if you had a choice.

I fear what awaits me. What disease has been haunting my mind and feeding off my body, consuming a banquet of healthy cells? Perhaps I've done in my liver, which no doubt has been punching the overtime clock for months.

A nurse I'd love to thank has exactly the right amount of professional calm and human kindness to take care of me, telling me precisely what's happening and what she and the doctors intend to do. Something like this has been going around, she explains. It's comforting to know hundreds of other people are also nauseated, dehydrated, depressed, drugged, exhuming their pasts, and paying the price.

At least I'm not alone.

Alas, four hours, two and a half IVs, a shot of Compazine, Benadryl, and a prescription for eight generic Xanax later, I'm on the road to recovery.

That night I sleep through the darkness for the first time in weeks. Although I'm still haunted by the dead of my past, the Xanax dulls the spectral visits. With my immune system back in working order, I should be able to stay ahead of the demons.

At least I hope so.

I understand this was a minor ailment. A couple of different strains of the flu bug. All my children and most other people I know have been through far worse. My wife and I have a daughter with failing kidneys and a host of rare neurological problems. She has suffered like few people I know. The depths of my dis-ease are not what concern me or this story. It's the aftermath.

By Tuesday morning of spring break, two days after the hospital and three days after having destroyed the drugs and used up the Xanax, I'm weak but feeling well enough to begin worrying – worrying about life as a clean man once again, worrying about how I'm going to deal with the dead hand of my personal history. Soon the court jesters of my past pick up where they left off. After a brief respite, my anger and depression have resumed gnawing at my fresh spate of health and hope.

I see no way out. I know drugs won't work in the long run. At forty-five I'm not going to drag myself into a therapist's office whining about all I haven't resolved of my past.

And then something happens.

Although it's not my custom to believe in old time religion or divine signs, something happens to me that I cannot fully explain.

By midweek I'm essentially feeling a semblance of the person I once was. Grateful for my returning health and for the absence of chemicals in my body, I keep things simple. I try to concern myself with nothing except what to do next. I give my dog fresh water and food and walk her twice a day. I answer the phone one out of every five or six times it rings; I heed every one of nature's calls. I sip ginger ale and eat saltines. I turn the lights on during the day and off at night. This I can handle.

And then one ordinary March afternoon a day or two later, I take my dog for a longer walk than usual. I need to get outside. My body and mind seem on the mend. I have successfully pushed away all thoughts of Tom, my mom, and the countless other dead of my life. I concentrate on nothing but the weather and landscape that surround me.

I listen to the snow squeaking beneath my feet and the geese honking overhead. I hear an Amish horse and buggy in the distance. As the buggy approaches, I'm stunned by the aesthetics of the black horse breathing vapor against the background of a snow-laden field. Having lived for fourteen years in an area of rural Ohio dense with Old Order Amish, I've seen horses and buggies hundreds of times. But something's different.

In the next moments, every ordinary sight and sound bursts with beauty. How could I have missed seeing how beautiful is an Amish horse in a nimbus of winter vapor? Have the clip-clopping hooves always dripped with such exquisite harmony? How could I not have noticed the beauty of a red tractor stalled in a dormant cornfield? For a second it feels again as if I might be dying. Is this the light some people claim to see before they die? Have the bare branches of an oak tree scratching against a winter sky always exuded such beauty? Down the road I can make out tiny clusters of black-clad angels scurrying against the snow. The sight of these Amish children walking home from school nearly drops me to my knees. The cold wind against my face feels like a frigid grace. An old man in a beat-up blue pickup passes me and waves. When he smiles a "how you doing on a typical cold winter afternoon in the new now" smile, my body seems to fill with love. It's as if something has revealed a tear in the surface of things. I see connections everywhere. The guy in the truck and the black-clad angels and the wind on my face and the tractor stalled in a winter-spent cornfield are all of one thing. It's as if I can reach through the hole in the surface of life and see how everything's held together. The beauty of it all shocks me still. It's as if I've seen into eternity. I at once understand the words of Thomas Merton: "Eternity is the present. Eternity is in the palm of the hand. Eternity is a seed of fire, whose sudden roots break barriers that keep my heart from being an abyss."

Soon an awesome global beauty simultaneously rises up and descends upon me. Every cell of my body burns and glows with a love and beauty I can barely withstand. I look around me, certain I'll see some gigantic presence looming in the winter afternoon. Turning in circles as if I'm being watched by an unseen intruder, I search for the cosmic body of love and beauty that is life. Everything comes alive. I'm enveloped in concentric circles of a force whose power I never knew existed.

In the next moment I'm aware of something bursting within. It's as if a box inside me has been smashed open and the contents rush to the surface; as if everything in there has been locked down for a thousand years and can't wait a nanosecond longer. Some kind of spiritual gravitational pull is at play.

Where has this beauty been hiding? I feel as if I need to bellow this beauty. So I do. I scream. I scream again. No words come out, just an elemental, primitive, joyful hollering to the hills.

This is outside the boundaries of my experience. I'm without words to describe it. I have nothing to measure it against.

My personal deus ex machina.

This has to be the love I've never really believed in. The love of the Creator. God's love.

And then a sort of liquid knowledge seeps into me: It's okay that I've outlived my mother. I deserve to live as much as anybody. Let Tom's death be the death that gives me new life.

I have already considered what happened to be the product of severe "welcome back to health you lucky bastard" ebullience, but it lasted too long for it simply to have been this euphoria. It came in a series of complicated waves day after day, and it still continues. Nor was it euphoria's distant, no-good, lying pseudocousin: God, if you get me out of this I swear I'll . . . No, not that either. Nor was it neurotransmitters or endorphins. I've experienced all of these highs and many others. Never have I known anything like this. Never has any experience lasted so long. Never before have I mutated so completely as a man.

As I stand there in the snow, suddenly aware that I'm somehow in the middle of a prayer, that the simple act of seeing beauty is a prayer, my mind's eye witnesses the stuff of my life go up in one form and come down in another, the way a cartoon doghouse explodes, rises in pieces, and then lands as a perfectly working grandfather clock.

I now believe this was nothing more than the descent of grace, God's love and beauty, some version of Paul's great glimpse. Whatever it was, it was nothing less than a wake-up call for a life half lived.

I had a comfortable, productive life before trying to exhume my past. As a tenured professor who works all of thirty weeks a year, I know I have it good. As a writer and an editor, I have work I love. I also share a fairytale love with the best woman I've ever met, and I have three great kids, fine relatives, and valued friends.

And yet. And yet . . .

I now know somehow I was not enough. I had enough, if Americans can ever have enough, but I simply *was* not enough.

Even with a good life, bouts of depression bored through my prescription Zoloft, leaving me wondering what the fuck any of us were doing on this bludgeoned and bloody planet. For months over the past twenty years, I had walked around in states of inebriation and depression even while fortune favored my endeavors.

Blaming my mother's early death and the other deaths that seemed to plunder my extended family before I even graduated from college, I accepted my dark views and cynical disposition as part of my spiritual DNA.

Well, my spiritual DNA was being manipulated.

Wanting to see this new truth for as long as I can, I vow to stay outside until my dog seems cold. A minute or so later, Sophie begins to shiver, so I turn us around and head for home. Never have my senses been so alive. And it isn't just that I can smell and see and touch and taste and hear as never before; it's also that everything I can smell and see and touch and taste and hear works as a conductor of God's love.

Moments later, just after Sophie and I walk in the back door, I begin seeing a picture in my mind's eye. It's the picture of a small boy sitting on a couch. I haven't thought about this old photo in years and have looked at it only once or twice in my entire life, but I see it now, and I need to see it again, right away.

I understand all at once and immediately that I have somebody to answer to. The boy I once was deserves an answer. I'm looking into his eyes as he stares back at me through the years. He's wearing a vertically striped shirt, and his pants have two penny-sized plastic buttons on the waist. With hands on his lap – ordered no doubt – one on each leg, one having probably just pushed to the side strands of brown hair with a white spot, he faces the camera with lips forming a smile, making it look like he's swallowed his teeth and is keeping it a secret. Apparently his mother or father or the family photographer has demanded he stop laughing. The couch he sits on may as well be a cavern or a mountain the way it dwarfs him. It's a fine little face he has. A fine little face. Intelligent, curious eyes. They're actually beaming. Because of the camera and the flash, of course, but because of something else too: his perfect pupils hold spots of white; his retinas beam, two tiny beacons against the brown of his eyes. He looks aware of life's sweet beauty and mystery. And he wants some of it. A lot of it. I'm not sure I've given him his wish.

He doesn't seem to be asking me anything. He looks at me as if he knows he's entitled to a blessed future – it's assured; he's confident of this. I admire his confidence in me and his hope, but . . . But when the man looks into the eyes of the boy he was, those eyes look back in all the photo's black-and-white beauty, and still they hope. Still they hope I will not disappoint. I will not squander, not for an instant, the gifts this boy has been given and does not yet realize he has.

When I look into my long-ago eyes, I start to cry. I know in my heart I have disappointed "the boy I once was and nowadays see little of," as E. B. White wrote.

This boy would never ingest poisons, nor would he ever surrender or betray, nor would he ever judge, or damn, or despair, nor would he ever leave wrapped a single, amoeba-sized gift.

I love this fucking kid. Here's the problem. Somewhere in the forty years since this photograph, I stopped loving the boy on the cavernous couch. Or perhaps I forgot he ever existed. I know he did. Somewhere in the intervening years I forgot this little boy with the fine thin face. I forgot or ignored or did not understand that the boy was I and I was he. He me and me he. I and I. I then and I now. No matter the years, no matter all the nors.

I want some of this boy back. I am forty-five years old now, forty years removed from the boy with the white birthmark in his hair, and in a room in a home I love with a family I love, I still cry for all that was given to me and for all he wants to give me. All I want from him. All he has been given. All I want to discover about us both before it's too late.

Every time I look over at him, he beams back the look. The love of God and humankind is in this child on the couch. He knows he will live forever even as he fears his death. I believe he has reappeared after forty years to teach me something I still have to learn before I die. Or rather, before I go on living. Before I can go on living. What encompasses that something is too much to grasp. I have not solved the mystery. I have a strong suspicion that his lessons are about love and grace and beauty and how they're everywhere and how I may go blind if I don't begin seeing them everywhere. Seeing them again, I should say. Seeing them for the first time again. Seeing them again for the first time.

I look away and then back, and the beaming boy I once was beams still. I see no signs of the dark side in the boy. There is no sadness hidden behind his smile. No deep cynicism. No misanthropy. No anger. No irony. I see no signs of depression either. I notice that his shirt collar sits askew and his right eye – lid and all – appears smaller than his left. I check to see if indeed my right eye has caught up in the intervening years. It has not. Thank God.

What this boy does after the photograph is taken I do not know. Perhaps he hops up and resumes the wild recklessness of five-year-old fun he'd been at before the forced pose. Perhaps he and his younger brother fight their way to the table at Grandma's for the first hot dog or the last cookie. Perhaps then he puts on his cowboy hat with his name stitched across the front and tightens the strings so it doesn't fall off or get stolen by his younger brother.

Whatever else I did that day is lost to time, of course. It's nice to believe that some parts of it are still somehow, somewhere, safe in that place where memory keeps even what it forgets, wrapped in wind like decades-old dust in a drafty attic. If they are safe in the place memory forgets, then there's a chance that other minutes of the day are stored in the memories of the family behind the camera.

Perhaps my dad was with us if the photo day fell on a holiday or a weekend. My mother is no doubt there. On a Valentine's Day fourteen years after the photo was snapped, she'd leave and take bits of that moment with her. If my paternal grandparents remembered the day their first grandchild had his picture taken on their couch, they've taken their memories with them. My grandfather left with his one snowy November evening not four years after this photo was taken; my grandmother toted hers away a dozen cold Novembers and a few winter months after that.

When his grandfather died, the boy in the photo cried for two days straight. I wonder if this was the beginning of the leaving.

I can still see myself lying across a bed in a maternal aunt's house – my parents were busy making funeral arrangements elsewhere – crying and refusing to come out of the room, unwilling to see or talk to anybody. When I look back now I believe my behavior was perhaps the purest form of grief I have ever felt. Here's why.

My father stopped in my bedroom late on the night his father died of his fifth heart attack while on a walk with his wife one snowy autumn evening just after supper. Dad gently shook me awake.

"How's Grandpa?" I asked.

"Grandpa's in heaven."

If my and my dad's memories are accurate, we hugged, my dad kissed me on the cheek, and I rolled over and fell back to sleep without a tear. I know that I believed those words "He's in heaven" so utterly, so naturally, so instinctively, the way I knew a pitched baseball would land, the way I knew streetlights shone at dusk, the way I knew my parents loved me. Whether my father believed them I cannot say for sure. I'm pretty confident he could not say those words now and truly mean them. My mother had the faith. My dad had faith in her and in their love. When she was gone, his faith seemed to take the trip with her.

As did mine. Until now.

So when I cried for two days on that bed, it was grief alone, untainted by fear or doubt, worry or wonder.

This is the grief I felt when I understood that I had been refusing or neglecting or denying or spurning the love of God. It took me decades to grieve purely again. Over the years I had grieved, but not purely, for my mother, my extended family, Tom, and others close to me. Now I could do that. Now I'm able to bask and believe.

When the sickly daughter I mentioned earlier was struggling in kindergarten, my wife and I met with her teachers. One teacher told us about an exercise they did where she'd begin by drawing part of a stick figure on a sheet of paper and asking the children to complete the drawing. She called it simply the incomplete man. Since I never let a chance of witty, self-deprecating, self-aware cynicism sneak by, of course I joked that the game was named for me.

Fifteen years after that day in my daughter's kindergarten, at forty-five years old, I understand the direness of the game's eponymous foretelling. A different child has shown me the way back to the everlasting job of completeness.

As is my custom, I am wrong about the reason for my return to the old neighborhood. I now know my search isn't really an attempt to discover the reasons for the ugly and early death of Tom McGinty. It isn't really about my mother's death. Maybe it isn't about death at all. Or perhaps it's about the power of life-giving death. Tom became my Jacob Marley. His death showed me my fate if I could not learn to accept the good life I deserve. In one sense Tom gave his life for me, so that I could see one future that surely awaited me if I kept on with the guilt and the shame and the drugs, the heavy emptiness of a life half lived.

I do know this journey has been about love. The love I believe God has for me. The love my mother went to her grave knowing.

Just weeks before this I would have shuddered with cynicism

and loathing at this whole notion. I would have ridiculed somebody who claimed to have experienced a moment of piercing the surface of things and being able to see, feel, touch, taste, and hear the giant quiet of divine love. I would have laughed at that person's simplicity. Hell, I'm laughing at my own! And yet as simple as it seems, it is simultaneously crushingly complicated.

When I realized I was in the throes of an awareness of God's love, I started an activity that gave me joy and a reconnection with something I hadn't thought about in forty years. And yes, it's laughable. From my recovery couch I began watching westerns. I'd have the Western Channel on half the day. Like a good many children of my generation, I loved Saturday and Sunday afternoon westerns. I loved the good guys and the bad guys, the cowboy and his horse. But what I remember loving more than anything was not something I would share with other western-watching boys. I loved the love angles. I loved the guy getting the girl and the girl getting the guy. Good, steady, loving men. Feisty, intelligent, pretty women.

I grew out of westerns, of course. I even resented them for years for all the reasons you already know. But more than three decades later, I lay on my couch, weeping through the love scenes like a love-sick idiot. And then I started crying during all acts of western love. If a man helped another man in need, I cried. When a woman gazed out a cabin window at an empty prairie, I cried. When a young girl blew out the flame of a kerosene lamp after saying goodnight to her family, I cried. When a man or woman cared for someone else's child, I cried. If a kid threw a dog a damn stick, I practically whimpered, and if the dog carried it back to the kid and received a pat on the head, my God . . .

If the scene was almost too beautiful, I would cry as if the landscape in the background of a two-star western were the most sublime vista on the planet.

I cried for love even though I have known it, owned it, felt it, felt secure in it, and given it my entire life. I am a lucky man who knows love.

This new knowledge of love was something different from any I've ever known.

When I wasn't studying photos or whimpering at westerns, I listened to the Beatles' "Here Comes the Sun" tens of times, maybe a hundred times in two or three days. I couldn't get enough of the happy hope the song promised.

Suddenly I felt young again. I had the joy of a child. And this was not nostalgia. I should know, because I'm vulnerable to its pull. I love nostalgia. I'm a card-carrying nostalgist. I've spent long moments swimming and swirling in its wet warmth. This was not it. The pain of nostalgia is the longing to return home when a return is impossible. I had no such unfulfilled longing. My return was assured.

I realized days later that this urge to enter love was a place I could indeed return to, although I never remembered being there or leaving there. It was the big love. The love with the capital *L* I'm afraid to use. Although I grew up Catholic, I've passed through atheism, agnosticism, and good old-fashioned secular humanism, yet I cannot call this anything other than the Creator Love I know it to be. The love of God. The love of which the boy on the couch was so surely possessed. It was the love that was there before he had language or tested intelligence or other intellectual tools for denying its existence.

What do you do when you have a great life – although you constantly complicate and diminish this great life – and then you are thrown into some understanding of a felt love that somehow reminds you what it was like before you could audibly articulate one crude and elementary desire? What do you do when you're suddenly made aware of the eternity in the now, of God's love on flesh and bone?

You accept it.

You nurture and nourish it.

You thank God for it.

You tether your soul to the truth Thomas Merton writes of, the truth that "there are drops of dew that show like sapphires in the grass as soon as the great sun appears, and leaves stir behind the hushed flight of an escaping dove."

I'd like to say that since my awakening, more than a year and a half ago now, I'm a completely changed person who sees only beauty, feels only love, knows nothing of rage or angst, depression or doubt, spends his days smothering strangers with all he now knows of love, and plans on quitting his job so he can personally feed the beaten, battered, and abused children of the world.

No can do.

As a matter of fact, just weeks after my great awakening I found myself in a nasty funk. Why? Because I wanted to see through the tear in the surface of things at any moment I chose. I wanted my version of Paul's glimpse again and again. I desired only – only! – to be able to flip my vision around on remote control, flipping past endless garbage until I came to rest on the Gigantic Glimpse of All Things Holy Channel. How come I can't see it today? I really need to see it. I felt like an insecure lover who needs to hear "I love you" every twenty seconds or he'll doubt his lover's love.

Just as I cannot take a drink without the knowledge that I'm a drunk, I cannot have despair-filled days without the precious knowledge that I once experienced and understood divine love.

For a while I had a hard time allowing this knowledge its natural and crucial need to move from the visceral to the intellectual. Doubt and depression descended as often as they always did, but they didn't stay. They knew they were no longer welcome. Perhaps there just wasn't any room for them. Faith fills.

There have been other developments as well. I'm once again a student of history. Now that I'm able to look beyond my own past, I've been able to rekindle my love of a history that is mine only in that I am a resident of that country, of that continent, of that planet. I'm able to understand that I'm a part of something bigger than my self, my solipsism having found a corner in which to slumber.

I'm also beginning to work with my hands again. My dad and I tore down my front porch the other day to make way for a new one. I loved the feel of a brick in my hand, of hardened mortar, of hammers and nails, of sun and dirt. My legs wore their working-class chemical burns with pride. My muscles ached for twenty-four hours, and the ache was welcome. The physical pain of labor returned like an old friendship, a friendship that ended years ago in a falling out over something neither friend can remember. Muscles indeed have memory. I'm not going to quit my academic job and become a bricklayer or carpenter. Hell, no builder in his or her right mind would hire me. But I'll at least think about doing a blue-collar job myself instead of reflexively hiring someone else. Living only in my mind can be a dangerous thing. The wholesale rejection of everything I once thought I was and thought I was not has cost me dearly.

I know I will never be complete by denying the things that make up who I am.

My relationship with the Catholic Church remains ambivalent and dubious. I love the rituals. I love the hymns. I love the groans the pews in an empty church make as the wood expands. I love being able to say "I'm Catholic" when somebody asks about my spirituality – it usually shuts people up in a hurry. They figure either you're recovering from Catholicism or you're a filthy papist sheltering pedophile priests. Either way, I can avoid having to discuss the sticky and uncertain matter of my fledgling faith. I loathe many of the church's rules and many of its rule enforcers, its exclusivity and damnable judgments. But despite all this, it feels comfortable now, welcoming, like home, in a way it never did before.

I still don't attend church on Sundays, although I may sneak into a service during the week. A house of worship with two or three strangers praying inside is my church of choice. But I'm aware of God's love everywhere. I see it in the prayerful underbelly of a hawk riding the thermals. I hear it in the sound of my dog lapping water out of her bowl – the small, sacramental splash of a thirst quenched, an elemental need met. I feel it in the touch of a passerby on a clogged street corner. I taste it in the acid-holy moisture of rain on my tongue. I smell it in the ancient freshness of dug-up earth.

I know this: I'll never let anything, particularly organized religion, interfere with my faith. I will never again feel guilty for living a good life. I will never again fantasize the oblivion of "self-administered overdose."

Not ever again.

I still run for cover when I hear people shouting their Christianity. I'd still like to beat all TV evangelists about the head and neck. I still raise my internal threat level to orange whenever I hear "praise" and "Allah" in the same sentence.

On my worst days, I have to fight the urge to smash my Volvo into the rear of a car with bumper stickers claiming the driver is saved and will revel in the Rapture as the rest of us burn in hell.

But on my best days I thank my mom, Tom, the numerous deaths of my extended family, and Fairlawn Drive for pulling me back, drawing me in, shaking me up, and then letting me go.

Letting me go.

My love of all things story has brought me full circle. Perhaps a life lived in literature has granted me the glory of finally being able to believe the greatest story ever told, in all its utter incredibility.

When I think back on the last street before Cleveland, I want all of the old neighborhood, all of the confused, ignorant boys who are now men, all of these perpetually pubescent blue-collar boys who hated kneelers and loved spitting, to know that grappling with the unknowable should never end; that this life should always be a battle between what is and what could be, between here and there, spiritual and corporeal, past and future, and ultimately, unbelief and belief, all examined through the sweet, brief window of the in between.

ACKNOWLEDGMENTS

I'd like to begin by thanking the folks on and around the last street before Cleveland, especially Rick Holland, Dave Rinella, Mary Maloney, and the entire McGinty family, in particular Ruthanne and Maryann.

Thanks to my early readers Brian Doyle, Elizabeth Frost-Knappman, Lee Martin, Mike Steinberg, and especially my good friend and mentor, and one of the best people I know, Dan Lehman.

I also owe thanks to master craftsman Bruce Harris for building and rebuilding me a place to write, to Dr. David Massie, and to Cleveland civil rights lawyer Avery Friedman.

Huge thanks to the dedicated pros at the University of Nebraska Press and to every writer's dream editor and advocate, the exquisite Ladette Randolph.

To my children, Jenny, Katy, and Dan, for teaching me what it means to be a father, I love you.

And to Dandi, my best friend, biggest supporter, and first reader – my bride, the best wife any guy could be lucky enough to have, the finest woman I know – thanks for the love of a lifetime, honey. I love you.

In the Class in America series

Cover Me: A Health Insurance Memoir
Sonya Huber

The Last Street Before Cleveland: An Accidental Pilgrimage
Joe Mackall

To order or obtain more information on these or other
University of Nebraska Press titles, visit www.nebraskapress.unl.edu.

CPSIA information can be obtained at www.ICGtesting.com
Printed in the USA
BVOW08s0239060314

346819BV00001B/1/P